For Life Is a Journey

4/27/2010

Bob and Ruthann

with great appreciation
for your friendship and
support.

Love
Ralph

For Life Is a Journey

Reflections on Living

Ralph G. McFadden

"Let each new temple, nobler than the last,
Shut thee from heaven with a dome more vast,
Till thou at length art free,
Leaving thine outgrown shell by life's unresting sea."

Oliver Wendell Holmes

Order this book online at www.trafford.com
or email orders@trafford.com

Most Trafford titles are also available at major online book retailers.

Printed in Victoria, BC, Canada.

ISBN: 978-1-4269-2790-4

*Our mission is to efficiently provide the world's finest, most comprehensive book publishing
service, enabling every author to experience success. To find out how to publish your book, your
way, and have it available worldwide, visit us online at www.trafford.com*

Trafford rev. 3/2/2010

 www.trafford.com

North America & international
toll-free: 1 888 232 4444 (USA & Canada)
phone: 250 383 6864 ♦ fax: 812 355 4082

For Kongkeo Xayavongvane,
my loving companion

Contents

Foreword

There is something captivating about a full throated, passionate voice that is deeply grounded and brazenly hopeful, despite being well tested.

Ralph McFadden came of age in a time when there were no positive gay role models. Homosexuality was hidden in a cloud of shame, and those who became visible could be charged with a crime, diagnosed with a mental illness, fired from their employment, and/or shunned by church and family. Like most people who were gay or lesbian, Ralph tried to do the "right" thing by getting married, having children, working hard, and denying himself. His gifts of leadership and management were recognized by his faith community, the Church of the Brethren, and for many years he served in various positions of influence on the local, district and national levels.

But there came a time when Ralph realized that for him it was no longer feasible to be out to himself and his family, yet remain publicly closeted. His desire for authenticity and transparency began to outweigh the benefits of status and position, and Ralph eventually made the courageous decision to push past his own internalized homophobia and move into a new and unexplored space of living as an openly gay man.

For Life is a Journey is Ralph's reflections about claiming his identity as a gay man and "surfacing his soul." He is honest about the depth of grief and anger that accompanied the changes that he was forced to make in terms of work, his marriage, family and friends. Of particular note is the sense of incredulous betrayal and abandonment that he experienced when the Church that had so profoundly shaped his commitments to peace, reconciliation, justice, now callously rejected him. Yet as Ralph notes, "in the struggling, the discovering, and the exploring came rebirth, reinvention, and reorganizing."

Ralph's nautilus journey led him to new professional experiences as an AIDS hospice chaplain and counselor, as well as new personal experiences like being partner to Keo, board chair of the Brethren Mennonite Council for LGBT Interests, and a gay activist. We are enriched by his stories of healing and growth in these areas. In addition, his move from a position of insider to that of outsider has placed him in a unique location to assess and critique leadership. Here, he speaks with the voice of a prophet as he challenges his church to be revolutionary and bold.

In his writing, Ralph is probably at his strongest when he reflects on the internal changes that have occurred as a result of his journey towards authenticity and truth. His honesty and emotional awareness are the marks of integrity and clarity. Coming out as a gay man was the main impetus for his particular experience, but his reflections invite each of us to consider the state of our own spiritual wellbeing and our own commitment to an authentic life. For that invitation and gentle challenge, I am indeed grateful.

Carol Wise, Executive, Brethren Mennonite Council for Lesbian, Gay, Bisexual, Transgender Interests

Preface: A Note to the Reader

Yes, I was angry. I was a former church executive and now was public about being a gay man with a partner. I wanted some of our church leaders to give serious attention to their attitudes and actions about sexual orientation. I decided that it would be wise and helpful to write from my own life and experience.

The first reflections went to a list of national and district staff and board members about five years ago. I had received a little response – but not much. Then it seemed like a good idea to write additional reflections and modify the earlier ones. In 2008 and 2009 I sent out a total of nine articles. These went via email to about 240 leaders: national and district staff, board members and over 30 pastors. I also included my family, many friends and others I considered on the more progressive side – biblically and theologically. I have received over 40 supportive and thoughtful responses. I noted, when talking to a friend recently, that I can identify only a couple national or district staff persons that responded in written word. Several said something to me in person. Generally that was "thank you for including me on your list."

Why, now, do I continue to write?

I am doing it for myself. I want to get my thoughts down. Simply that. For my own sake. I want and need to express my feelings, my doubts, my anxieties, my concerns, and my opinions. There are some stories, poetry and humorous anecdotes. My experience is that the process of writing and putting down my thoughts is good for my Soul. Taking time to sit quietly and write seems to be a salve when my spirit is broken and an encouragement to move toward a life of wholeness and fulfillment. To find a quiet place to write is in itself soothing. The local library and Siloam, a retreat hermitage not far from Elgin, have been the best places.

And I continue to write for others. I want to influence folks when it comes to lgbt persons: more understanding, significant and supportive decisions, and the hope for a more promising future. Actually, this is a very strong feeling.

This book is written for a broad audience. You may be from another denomination or no denomination, yet I think there may be some insights that will be helpful in your own journey.

Sometimes I simply want people to know of the excellent lgbt persons that are in the church and in their lives. I want you as a reader to think about what it might mean to become an open and affirming person and congregation. I want to encourage you to be supportive of your friends and families who are allies. I wish for those of you who are on a journey of discovery about your own sexual orientation that you will find *shalom* - peace.

You may note, as a reader, that there is an occasional repetition of ideas, quotes and anecdotes. And there will be inconsistency. These reflections were written over a period of years for different events and audiences. And, I remind myself, I am on a journey. Always on a journey. You will find that there are interspersed throughout the book, in the midst of the advocacy reflections, poems, letters to friends, and stories. They are a part of my journey. I hope you will enjoy the side-bars.

I encourage you to respond to the concerns raised in this book. And you may copy any of the material and share it with others.

One further note at this point: in terms of support for the rights of lgbt persons, the church culture is far behind our general culture. For instance, in the past we in the Church of the Brethren have taken the lead on freeing slaves, supporting civil rights, encouraging women in leadership, and seeking peace at all levels: international, national and in our denominational and private lives. We are strong in supporting environmental concerns. We have acknowledged and have tried to work at domestic violence and sexual, physical and mental abuse. The list goes on.

The pattern has not held when it comes to the humanity of persons who happen, by God's grace, to be lesbian, gay, bisexual or transgender. Fortunately, some of the major Protestant denominations are moving ahead. I am thankful for that encouragement. The Church of the Brethren was unique in its historic peace witness. Now other denominations have also become peace advocates. And others have become advocates for the rights, equality, and humanity of lgbt persons.

Personally, some of my recent life experience has determined my wish to push harder on this 'homosexual agenda.' (Now isn't that an interesting indictment by the religious right? That name-calling is spoken as though only we have an agenda.) In 2002 I was diagnosed with a life threatening disease – ITP - Immuno thrombocytopenic purpura. * I have been hospitalized five times with ITP – and in the summer of 2008 spent 40 days in the hospital with a serious infection likely having to do with my compromised immune system.

There is a wonderful book, "How, Then, Shall I Live" by Wayne Muller. He asks, "Knowing that I shall die, how then shall I live?" That is my focus also: Knowing that, hopefully, I shall live for a few more years, how then shall I live?

That thought helps me summarize the intent of my writing. I do want an outcome. Because of this writing I hope that some of you will be nudged or pushed or encouraged to move progressively into responding positively on issues of justice including lgbt concerns. It is not enough to be silently supportive. It is simply not enough.

Ralph G. McFadden, February 2010

* See Glossary

Acknowledgments

For almost 40 years, my many friends in Brethren Mennonite Council have encouraged me to be open, championed my audacity at being outspoken, been patient with my uncertainty about being 'out,' and in the final analysis, simply loved me.

My family and many friends have greatly enriched my life with their respect, love, and support. Yes, there have been some uncertainties, but those relationships have been a positive undergirding that encourages me to live life fully.

Keo, my loving partner, has put up with me: attaching myself to the computer, focusing on the next steps, and being bodily transported to the library and the retreat Siloam hermitage. Keo is a constant source for energizing my Soul's well being.

BMC executives Jim Sauder and Carol Wise have my heartfelt appreciation for their constancy in giving direction to BMC, to me, and to all of us in our 'coming out' journeys. Martin Rock, the founder of BMC, has been a source of strength by his example of courage and advocacy.

The initial phase of this book was writing and sending out ten "reflections" to about 240 friends, asking that they give attention to the difficult and sometimes extreme challenges facing lgbt (lesbian, gay, bisexual and transgender) folks living in a hostile societal and church culture. I thank the several dozen persons who responded to those reflections expressing their appreciation and encouraging me to continue writing.

Many friends have been very supportive as they encouraged me to continue in my writing. They include Martha Bartholomew, Carol Wise, Joel and Donna Kline, Audrey deCoursey, Moses Mason, Jesse Hultstrand, Ben and Mandy Brobst-Renaud, Verlyn Barker, and Anna Speicher.

I thank Todd Flory who gave early assistance as a copy editor. The current copy editing and editing has been the excellent work of Audrey deCoursey. They helped to correct my grammar and spelling, and made suggestions that filled in the gaps in my thought process. The words are always my own. And I take final responsibility for any missteps.

Ben Brobst-Renaud is the artist for the nautilus sketches found in the book. It was Ben's suggestion that repeated use of the sketches would remind the reader of the continuous journey of our lives.

Journey of the Nautilus

The picture on the cover page is of a Chambered Nautilus. This mollusk is a unique member of the cephalopod family. The nautilus reproduces by laying eggs that are usually attached to rocks in shallow water. These eggs require between eight to twelve months to fully develop. When a young nautilus first hatches from its egg, it is about an inch in diameter and has a shell with seven chambers. As it gets larger, it will add new chambers to the shell. Each chamber will be a little larger than the last. The nautilus moves into the new chamber to continue its life.

Fascinating! The living nautilus moves on in its journey by moving into a new and larger chamber. Oliver Wendell Holmes writes of the nautilus; "He left the past year's dwelling for the new . . . Stretched in his last-found home, and knew the old no more." He continues; "Build thee more stately mansions, O my soul, /As the swift seasons roll, /Leave thy low-vaulted past."

What a wonderful metaphor! In each day and year of our lives we build a new chamber. We move ahead on our journey by moving into that new unknown promise. Our life existence and experience is in moving ahead, not in staying behind. If we do not build a new chamber and try to stay in the old, we are fatally locked into that "secure cocoon" and eventually are so chained and shackled that we are eventually squeezed to death by the confines of the past. Perhaps not a bodily death, but a spiritual death.

And yet it is also true, as a friend pointed out to me, that in the transition into that new chamber – that new space - it is taking a risk. It becomes vulnerable to its predators. Its very flesh is now out there for its enemies to see and attack.

We may not live up to the spirit of the ancient nautilus, but the challenge is there. Move into a new and yet unexplored space. Risk the unknown future.

For the nautilus, the past is always present there on its back. However, that heavy shell's chambers are filled with air. A tiny hole in each chamber allows the nautilus to infuse air into those caverns. The potentially heavy home of the nautilus becomes almost weightless. The past is not a burden. The memories of the past, of joy and suffering, help to define our lives not only now, but also for the future.

"Let each new temple, nobler than the last, /Shut thee from heaven with a dome more vast, /Till thou at length art free, Leaving thine outgrown shell by life's unresting sea."

Ben's* sketches of the Chambered Nautilus throughout the book are, for me, the consistent reminder that life is, indeed, a journey - a Soul journey.

* Ben Brobst-Renaud

The Chambered Nautilus

This is the ship of pearl, which, poets feign,
    Sails the unshadowed main,
    The venturous bark that flings
On the sweet summer wind its purple wings
In gulfs enchanted, where the Siren sings,
    And coral reefs lie bare,
Where the cold sea-maids rise to sun their
    streaming hair.

Its webs of living gauze no more unfurl,
    Wrecked in the ship of pearl!
    And every chambered cell,
Where its dim, dreaming life was wont to dwell,
As the frail tenant shaped his growing shell,
    Before thee lies revealed, -
Its irised ceiling rent, its sunless crypt unsealed!

Year after year beheld the silent toil
    That spread his lustrous coil,
    Still, as the spiral grew,
He left the past year's dwelling for the new,
Stole with soft step its shining archway through,
    Built up its idle door,
Stretched in his last-found home,
    And knew the old no more.

Thanks for the heavenly message brought by thee,
    Child of the wandering sea,
    Cast from her lap, forlorn!
From thy dead lips a clearer note is born
Than ever Triton blew from wreath'ed horn!
    While on mine ear it rings
Through the deep caves of thought
    I hear a voice that rings: -

Build thee more stately mansions, O my soul,
    As the swift seasons roll!
    Leave thy low-vaulted past!
Let each new temple, nobler than the last,
Shut thee from heaven with a dome more vast,
    Till thou at length art free,
Leaving thine outgrown shell by life's unresting sea!

Oliver Wendell Holmes   1809 – 1894

For Life Is a Journey

In his book "How, Then, Shall We Live?" Wayne Muller quotes a woman who was taught by her family that she ought to be ashamed because she was not white. She said,

> If we feel ashamed of who we are, we will pretend to be someone else. In the process of trying to satisfy these demands, to be someone else, we do great harm to our natural sense of self. When we struggle to create a new persona that is less offensive and more pleasing, acting the way they want us to be, just to feel safe, acting this way over and over and over, each day, year after year - in time we begin to forget who we are.[1]

In 1969 I 'came out' as a gay man to Barbara, my wife. I do not think that I had expected, as I ventured into this new area of my life, 'coming out,' that I would experience such grief and loss. Perhaps I thought that it would change my life. But what was unexpected was how much it would change my very being.

I had told Barbara when we lived in Maryland. And Barbara and I told our children one Christmas vacation in the late 70's when Joel was in graduate school and Jill was at a university that I was bisexual or gay. We were still married, and we stayed together until the mid-90's. And even though I was aware of my sexual desires, I did not act on them, only spoke of them. During the years of the 70's and 80's I told a few friends, then, one Thanksgiving, 1989, I told my extended family.

---

1   *How, Then, Shall We Live?* Wayne Muller, 1996, Bantam Books

The primary and most intense focus of 'coming out' to myself and to others was in 1988 and 89 when I was in Clinical Pastoral Education (CPE) * - a yearlong chaplain training residency program at Rush Presbyterian-St. Luke's Medical Center in Chicago. It was then that I began to realize that coming to terms with myself would mean tremendous loss. I said mid-way into that year that I would no longer take a job in which I could not be open if I wished. I knew that decision would very likely end my professional career with my denomination, the Church of the Brethren. And I cried. I grieved. I recall one time, during supervision, when, in order to vent my anger and to make clear my feelings toward the church, I asked John, one of my colleagues, to stand on a chair, and I stood beneath him, and crying, shouting and shaking my fist, I bellowed out my anger and my grief.

I think that I also knew, though it was not spoken, that there was an inevitability about this coming out, that it would mean something life changing for work, for my marriage and for my family. That was so. And though the coming out was a matter of integrity, freedom, and a new and adventuresome path, it was also a matter, over months and years, of tremendous loss — of friends, of job possibilities, of verbal abuse and emotional violence, and even the respect and caring of others.

Following my chaplaincy residency, I was hired as a chaplain with Hospice of Metro Denver. There I began to learn about the nature of grief, its impact, the journey through grief, and the rediscovery of new life. I also began to learn, working with men, women and children with AIDS, and with partners, families, and friends, of the fear, dread, hostility, and rejection around AIDS and of those who were gay. Much of that negative response I witnessed came from Christians. When it started, I cannot say precisely. But I began to experience a growing mistrust of and anger with the church.

A part of this anger and grief was the awareness that the church was not behaving like I had expected it to behave. I had been tremendously naive. I am a born and bred Brethren. I have a history with the church believing that it was deeply immersed in justice, reconciliation and peace.

My father and mother taught me about compassion, peace, reconciliation and justice. We had Japanese-Americans in our home in the early 40's when it was very unpopular. The church in Troy, Ohio, where Dad was pastor was one of the first in the Church of the Brethren to have a 'Negro' family as members. My father was on the cutting edge of open housing in Elgin, Illinois, in the early 50's when he was pastor there.

I learned something of working on justice and reconciliation when I sat on the Mayor's Human Relations Council in Lafayette, Indiana, when I worked in Washington, DC with other denominational judicatory executives on the Poor People's campaign and the race riots, when I lobbied for our congregation to become a sanctuary for Central American refugees, when I was on the international board of the Brethren Mennonite Council for Lesbian, Gay, Bisexual, and Transgender Interests, and when, as a church executive, I tried to bridge the gap between the evangelicals, fundamentalists, feminists, gays/lesbians and the denominational headquarters. I especially learned something about integrity, openness, compassion, reconciliation, and justice when I decided to come out as a gay man to my family, friends, and to the church.

In time, I came to realize that even an historical peace church can be deeply mired in self-preservation, and can be very cautious about taking a stand on controversial issues. It may grieve its inability to face up to and take action with these issues that some know to be concerns of justice - but the church, for the most part, remains hostile and inhospitable to the journey of gays and lesbians, and to sexual orientation as a justice issue. For my friends in the church who claim to understand and to love me and others who are lgbt, the reality is often that economics, church unity and church politics speak louder than the need for truth, justice, reconciliation.

For me, the church has caused horrendous grief, pain and loss. I ask, "Where is the courage? Where is the vision?" Karl Jung speaks of each of us having a 'shadow side.' There is a shadow side to the church.

The good thing for me about coming out and being gay is the sad, depressing, dreadful and sometimes overwhelming struggle I have undergone has helped me to become this unique person that I am. To be challenged, to come out to myself, and to come out to others has taken courage, heart, and energy, which have ultimately resulted, I believe, in a very high degree of integrity. I have had to learn what it is to be authentic and genuine. And denominations and congregations will need to go through the same struggles of coming out into the open as they support lgbt persons. It will take courage, heart and energy.

As the chasm deepened between me and the church, as the sorrow of being rejected increased, as the struggle and pain often seemed to put me occasionally into a low grade depression, there was, nonetheless, a beginning discovery of Self.

Muller writes: "Within the sorrow, there is grace. When we come close to those things which break us down, we touch those things that also break us open."

Struggle, discovery and reinvention are a part of my story. It is a story the church needs.

In coming out, after the first awareness of grief and loss, there has been a middle time in this journey, a time of valuing, of remembering, of bargaining, of ruminating, of cursing, of being stunned, disbelieving, and of being incredulous. It can be, and was for me, not only a time of intense feelings of disbelief, agony, and pain, but also a time of discovery -- a rethinking about life.

In this middle time of reevaluating, feeling anger, mistrust, and uncertainty, I was aware of something else Muller said: "How many of us are secretly waiting for some magical permission - like a diagnosis of terminal illness - before we truly begin to listen to the quiet dreams, the desires of the heart?" In the struggling, the discovering, and the exploring came rebirth, reinvention, and reorganizing.

For me, once the journey started there has been a movement toward new life, hope, fullness, wholeness, and health - a journey that no longer includes self-destructive behavior.

To be out is to be strong, to be identified with integrity. Certainly there is still hurt, loss, and struggle. Yet there is also strength, insight, and affirmation of Self.

In grief work we sometimes used the term 'reinvent.' For me, to reinvent my life has meant opening the door to new ideas and new life options. I know that I cannot return to the old. And to be gay and to be on this journey is to know, absolutely know, that I cannot see life in the old way. The traditional and conservative views have to be encountered, evaluated, and revised. I am now on the outside of that old church culture, and I see with different eyes.

One of the redefinitions for me is *how I see and deal with the church*. It is difficult, still, for me to accept how quiet the church is in this controversy.

A national care-giving group that I worked with identified itself as a resource for those who are hurting, afraid, silent, and left at the margins. "Breaking down the dividing walls" and therefore being truly inclusive would mean building an alliance with those who are silenced - and those who are silent.

When it comes to these lgbt concerns, I cannot be silent. Neither can the church. It is time for the leaders of congregations and denominations to recognize that being quiet is an assault. Domestic violence, for instance, is not to be tolerated and congregations cannot be silent in the face of such violence. Moreover, merely not naming domestic violence is alliance with abuse; unless we are vocally opposed to it, we condone the cultural status quo that condones it.

It is my experience that violence by word and deed against gays and lesbians is tolerated. And to be quiet, I believe, is to be violent. I am often amazed that conservatives have a platform to speak out vociferously about homosexuality, but liberals and progressives, because they want to be respectful of all points of view, refuse to call out the cruel agenda of those who say they love the sinner, but not the sin. I wonder - - - is a silent ally really an ally?

Chuck Boyer, then a pastor of an open and affirming congregation in California, spoke at a BMC lgbt luncheon in 2001. He said,

> As we have become more inclusive of persons of color, divorced persons and women in leadership, we are also becoming more inclusive of lgbt (lesbian, gay, bisexual, transgender) people. The process is slow. We do not need to wait on an annual conference or a judicatory conference or the local congregations to act. The Church of the Brethren majority was wrong in categorically excluding African-Americans and other persons of color from membership and leadership. The Brethren majority was wrong in categorically excluding qualified divorced persons from leadership positions. The Brethren majority was wrong in categorically excluding women from leadership positions. The Brethren majority is wrong again in categorically excluding lgbt persons from leadership positions. This is not debatable!

I am thankful for the actions of my congregation, the Highland Avenue Church of the Brethren, over the years: for its support of open housing in the 50's, for becoming a sanctuary church for Central American refugees in the 70's, for encouraging persons who support peace initiatives and environmental health, for providing opportunity for women in ministry, and for the years of sacrificially supporting the homeless. The list of justice concerns is long: supporting conscientious objectors, resettlement of refugees, Habitat for Humanity, Heifer International, On Earth Peace, helping victims of domestic violence, soup kitchens, and so forth. These initiatives of support for justice have attracted people to the Highland Avenue congregation.

In May of 2009 the Highland Avenue congregation voted to become a part of the Supportive Communities Network, an ally organization of Brethren Mennonite Council for Lesbian, Gay, Bisexual and Transgender Interests. * You can read the supportive documents on the website of the congregation: www.hacob.org.

Many persons in our congregations are stating that it is time for congregations to put themselves on the line for civil and human rights for lesbian, gay, bisexual, and transgender men and women. It is time to become a publically affirming welcoming congregation, making certain that gays and lesbians in this church and community know - with no doubt - that they are welcome to worship, take leadership, become ordained in ministry, and have committed relationships blessed.

This journey is for me, and will be for you, at times, a struggle: unreal, unbelievable, inconceivable, incredible, incredulous, astounding, dismaying, shocking, frustrating, challenging, a gigantic learning experience, empowering, draining, hope-inspiring, enslaving, and freeing.

Do you recall the poignant scene in the film *"Philadelphia?"* Andy, played by Tom Hanks, dying with AIDS, is talking late at night with his attorney, played by Denzel Washington, holding on to his IV pole, and listening to Maria Callas singing about tragedy. Andy is caught in a trance of the soaring music, tears streaming down his face, interpreting the words from the Italian "La Mamma Morta:" "In all this sorrow, my poor heart woke to love." Or in another translation, "For out of sorrow comes love."

And out of sorrow comes strength, Self, a deepening of spirit, and compassion. I am sure that I have not learned enough from the sorrow. I realize that sometimes I have not learned love, or compassion, or deepening of the spirit. I am still on that journey, and it is and will be an endless journey. Yet, for me, it is better to be on the journey than to be sitting permanently in some highway rest area.

Once again, Wayne Muller: "The heart of most spiritual practice is simply this: Remember. Remember who you are. Remember what you love. Remember what is sacred. Remember what is true. Remember that you will die, and that this day is a gift. Remember how you wish to live."

* See Glossary

Epiphany at Epiphany

Epiphany, a sudden realization, a sudden intuitive leap of understanding,
especially through an ordinary but striking occurrence.

It was an epiphany moment for me. As is the practice in our congregation, the bread and cup communion was being offered on this first Sunday of Epiphany.

I have sometimes been indifferent about taking part in communion. But this day I decided that I was going to participate. As I moved, along with others, into the center aisle to go forward to receive communion, I suddenly remembered a time when I had been denied communion. And then it came to me and I realized with thankfulness that I now had the choice to "come to the table."

I recall vividly that time that I felt excluded. It was in the spring of my yearlong Clinical Pastoral Education residency in a Chicago hospital. My wife Barbara (we were still married at that time), our son Joel, his woman friend, and I were attending a Catholic university church located on the shore of Lake Michigan. It was Easter Saturday – the Easter Eve midnight mass.

I was in the midst of a rather difficult CPE year. I was beginning to realize that I would not be willing to return as an ordained professional to a position in my denomination unless I could be completely honest about my sexuality. I was struggling with my own integrity. And I was grieving because I understood that in all likelihood I would probably never again be a pastor in the Church of the Brethren, or a District Executive, or a national staff person. I was, I know, on an emotional edge.

11

Then, that late Saturday night in that lovely cathedral, as the Easter eve service was coming to a conclusion, the priest made it clear that *only* Catholics would be invited to the table. Though I was not Catholic, and though an invitation was not expected, I felt that I was being physically heaved out the door, and out of the church, even my own church. Reality struck. I was no longer welcome at the table, not even in my own denomination. I felt, deep in my soul, excluded and alone. And, on that quiet Easter eve, sitting with my family, I cried.

This past Epiphany Sunday (January 2009) I realized that our congregation – and I – had come a long, long way. We are now a congregation that welcomes gays and lesbians. I was, without rebuke and without question, invited to the table. The pastor was clear. All may come. And again, I cried.

I would wish that you could imagine what is going through the heart and soul of any person in your congregation who feels, openly or secretly, that the table is not open . . . that they are not welcome.

Some of those who may feel uninvited are persons who are gay, lesbian, bisexual, or transgender; persons with physical and mental disabilities; persons of color in an all-white congregation; those who feel undereducated; those without money; the homeless; the poor; the depressed; survivors of child abuse, women and men struggling with abortion, and those with a mental illness.

A congregation that faithfully, honestly, prophetically, and courageously seeks out what it means to be inclusive of gays and lesbians will also find that they are dealing with a whole new world of what it means to be inclusive to all. Conversely, the congregation that tries to include some but excludes others, such as gays and lesbians, still has not dealt forthrightly with what it means to present a welcoming table.

It is my belief that a truly welcoming congregation is a congregation that has courage. They have been willing to confront and talk in depth with those who are blatant excluders. It is an interesting dilemma, isn't it? It would appear that sometimes congregations exclude some from the table in order to keep the excluders who are within the congregation – in.

A mentor of mine, the late Benton Rhoades, at an event of lgbt persons, feminists, and allies, said that we, in our denomination, were reaching a "critical mass." Benton was prophesying that there is within the Church of the Brethren a nucleus that was moving the church toward becoming inclusive. Perhaps he was right. Several years ago over 200 supporters came to a "witness" event at our national church conference demonstrating support for Brethren Mennonite Council who had, once again, been denied an exhibit space at the conference. And in the following year two other progressive groups, in solidarity with BMC, decided not to have their own exhibit space. At the 2009 Annual Conference literally hundreds of conference goers wore rainbow scarves. The Womaen's Caucus sponsored the scarves that had been knitted and were given to conference goes to wear as a statement of support for lgbt inclusion.

What an incongruity! At our national conference it was somehow logical for conference planners to give visibility to a fundamentalist group, which in *many actions* did not agree with the statements of faith of our denomination, but would not recognize the Brethren Mennonite Council which in most of its concerns about justice, peace, and reconciliation had agreed with our denominational statements and resolutions on issues of justice, peace and reconciliation. What can we do? What can you do? What is needed is a *movement* of believers!

Write to the executives of your denominational agencies. Let your judicatory executives and boards know your opinion. Talk with your voting representatives. Have you written or spoken to some of the decision makers locally, regionally, or nationally? Have you spoken up in your own congregation? Have you made it clear – very clear – to those who may feel excluded that they are truly welcome to come to the table in your congregation?

When will you have your next God-sent epiphany moment?

> *The arc of history bends toward justice.*
> *Rev. Dr. Martin Luther King, Jr.*

Authenticity

A number of years ago, my daughter Jill introduced me to the words and music of Fred Small in a choral piece entitled "Everything Possible." Small writes,

> Oh, you can be anybody you want to be, you can love
>   whomever you will.
> You can travel to any country where your heart leads and
>   know that I will love you still.
> You can live by yourself, you can gather friends around,
>   you can choose one special one.
> And the only measure of your words and your deeds,
>   will be the love you leave behind when you're done.
>
> There are girls who grow up strong and bold,
> There are boys quiet and kind.
> Some race ahead, some follow behind, some go in their
>   own way and time.
> Some women love women, some men love men,
>   Some raise children, some never do.
> You can dream all the day never reaching the end of
>   everything possible for you.[2]

Some time ago in a moment of self-reflection, I wrote:
I like mashed potatoes and gravy.
>   I don't like having more cracks in our concrete
>   driveway.

---

[2]   *Everything Possible*, Words and Music by Fred Small, 1993

I like the deep colors of our fall mums. I prefer eggs over-
easy.
I'm glad that I graduated from Manchester
College.
Taking CPE (chaplain training) in my late fifties was
wonderful.
I love golden Aspen leaves in October in
Colorado.
I take my turn cleaning the bathrooms.
I try to do my taxes honestly.
I like my jeans when they are freshly laundered.
My handwriting is dreadful, especially compared
to my father's artistic penmanship.
I sometimes eat too much of the wrong stuff.
As I get older my singing voice wobbles more.

I'm pretty normal, right? So why am I identified as abnormal and sinful by some? Am I really that different?

During a recent board meeting of BMC, one of our board members said, "We are all different. There is no norm. There is only authenticity." He added, as we talked about BMC and the folks in churches making the decisions to try to keep the church from splitting, "Living needs to be authenticity over unity."

He was right. There is no norm. Being normal is okay, but only if it is understood that part of being normal is recognizing how different each one of us is. My challenge these days is to be, as much as possible, authentic. And, I ponder, what is it to be authentic? What is it, for me, to be real and genuine?

For me, to be authentic is a matter of not being in the closet, of not covering up, of not wearing a mask, of not being deceitful. Being authentic and genuine is more than what one says. It is more than the truthful use of words. Being authentic is the surfacing of one's Soul. Being authentic and genuine is being transparent.

To some folks being authentic may have the appearance of being arrogant, confrontational, unnecessarily truthful, too personal, rude, or insensitive to the experience of others.

As an aside, as I sit here at my laptop in a small village in Laos, I am a guest in a culture where transparency might be considered rude or embarrassing. As I write I realize that transparency, authenticity, and genuineness are, for me, all very personal traits.

Somewhere along the line, courage is needed to be authentic. What I believe must be clearly stated. Authenticity means speaking openly or sharing openly when the opportunity is there. And sometimes that is not easy.

At other times being authentic is being quiet. Or, another way of saying it, I am not willing to share all of what I believe – or feel – or desire – with everyone. There are times that I am silent.

In a reflection piece in the March 2007 Church of the Brethren *Messenger* Larry Brumfield writes,

> One of the most seemingly innocent but false statements perpetrated on the American public and particularly church folk, is that God doesn't see color. Color does not matter to God; God loves us all. The truth is God not only sees it, God made it. This is awesome. The same God who didn't fill the ocean with all blue fish, the same God who didn't fill the jungle with all white flowers is the same God who made many nations of different people. God not only sees color, he loves it. God loves the variety, the changes, the cultures.[3]

The article reminded me of my own uniqueness. I am, among a thousand other attributes, gay. And I believe the same truth that Brumfield believes, though I do not, of course, assume that he agrees with me. When it comes to being gay or lesbian, the truth is that God not only sees my uniqueness, but God made me. I celebrate the whole person that I am, who God loves.

One of the most difficult daily tasks for me, as a gay man in the church and in the culture, is to recognize my own homophobia. I have been taught by culture and church to hate myself. I have been indirectly taunted because I am not only "indisputably" different but also labeled sinful, immoral (is that redundant?), illegal, and mentally off-balance.

I have been angry with the church and its deeply biased and marred teachings, and its incredulous and diabolical indifference to gays and

---

3   Larry Brumfield, "Reflections," Church of the Brethren *Messenger*, March 2007

lesbians through inaction and unjust decision-making. The church must face its own struggles with authenticity and genuineness.

While the church, through articles, ads in church publications, bulletins, and sermons, celebrates diversity and justice and claims "all are welcome," it often slams the door shut. Can you imagine how angry and sad one becomes when the language is for openness and celebration, but the action is clearly closed? And progressive leaders sometimes close that door, I think, because of economics, Biblical interpretation, beliefs, and fear of conservative reprisals. It seems that it is okay to be very clear about Iraq, but very quiet and unclear about the injustice of the treatment of lgbt persons.

What did Fred Small write?

> Oh, you can be anybody you want to be, you can love
> whomever you will.
> You can travel to any country where your heart leads and
> know that I will love you still.
> You can live by yourself, you can gather friends around,
> you can choose one special one.
> And the only measure of your words and your deeds,
> will be the love you leave behind when you're done.

My Friend, Joseph Lee

Joe was a professor at an art school in Denver. When I met him he had been living with AIDS for five years. I met him in his last months, in a nursing home and under the watchful care of the staff of Hospice of Metro Denver. The early 1990s were a time when persons diagnosed with HIV quickly moved into a diagnosis of AIDS. And the expectancy was that death would soon follow.

I was a hospice chaplain. I had often visited that particular nursing home near downtown Denver. It was an okay place, old but clean. Very little odor of urine and sickness. Joe was on the second floor in the west wing. He shared a room with two other male patients.

I visited Joe twice a week. He had a good sense of humor and was well aware of city, state and national issues. I knew from what he had said that he enjoyed teaching and being an artist and a poet. He was 'spiritual' but no longer affiliated with a congregation. He had been 'booted out' or perhaps had chosen to disassociate with his rather conservative religious background. In the times that I visited him I never met a pastor or a friend from his former church.

I did meet Joe's daughter, Charlene. Joe, like so many of the men with AIDS that I met, had, at one time, been married. It was not unusual to be openly gay with a history of marriage and family. What was unusual was that on occasion family members would support the son, or father, or husband by visiting and providing care. Charlene was like that . . . a supportive, non-judgmental, visiting and caring family member. In part, I recall that because it was remarkable, and because I was always grateful when persons in hospice care had the support of family.

This brief story comes from one of the last times I visited Joe. He had been getting weaker and had lost a lot of weight. Most of the time, he was confined to his bed or to a wheelchair. He was often fatigued, but was still "of sound mind" and enjoyed talking about his life. He was not afraid of his coming death. He was still living even though he was dying. He had his sense of humor. He had the support of his family and friends.

I came into his room one sunny spring afternoon. He had finished his lunch and was sitting up in his wheelchair. We spoke of his waning health, his wishes for his family, and his thoughts about a memorial service. I was grateful that he was giving me and his family and friends an example of how to die with dignity.

Joe capped off that afternoon visit with a quip that still leaves me smiling. I was about to leave and he asked me to assist him in getting back into his bed. Not a problem. Even though he was almost 6 feet tall, by now he probably weighed only 85 pounds.

I went to his side, positioned the wheelchair beside the bed, and had him wrap his arms around my neck. I put my arms around his back and under his legs and slowly and carefully lifted him onto the bed. As I laid him down and he took his arms from around my neck, he sighed and said, "Oh, I think I'm in love again." And we laughed.

Later that week, he died.

I am thankful that I learned to know Joe. I was thankful for his positive outlook on living. I was thankful that his daughter asked me to conduct his memorial service. I was thankful that Hospice of Metro Denver encouraged support of patients – gay or straight. I wondered, at the time, why his church had not been present and visible in his life.

For that service Charlene gave me one of his poems to read: "This I Know." He wrote it after he had been diagnosed with AIDS and when he was aware of his impending death. I have his daughter's permission to share it with you.

This I Know

This I know:

I have planted a garden,
 so I know what faith is.

I have seen the tall trees swaying in the breeze,
 so I know what grace is.

I have listened to the birds singing,
  so I know what the joy of music is.

I have watched little children playing,
  so I know what entertainment is.

I have seen mornings without clouds, after showers,
  so I know what real beauty is.

I have seen the miracle of the sunset,
  so I know what grandeur is.

I have lived among family and friends,
  so I know what love is.

And because I have perceived all these things,
  I know what wealth is!

Leonard Joseph Lee,   1989

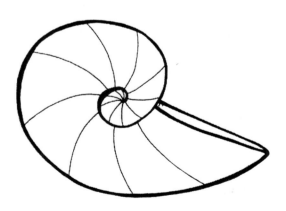

Silence about Injustice is, Itself, an Injustice

"Silence about injustice is, itself, an injustice." That's a powerful statement. This can be a difficult issue for many; it certainly has been difficult for me from time to time. In my own struggles about being gay, I have been quiet. Certainly in my early years as I became aware of my own sexuality I chose silence over "coming out" to family, friends and the church.

The years passed and I found that it was possible to share with the family, then with a few friends, and occasionally with a group of people, such as work colleagues.

Increasingly, I have made the choice to be vocal or to put my thoughts in writing. I believe when one is living with and experiencing injustice that at least one of the choices must be to speak out.

There are many injustices. Far too many. The rich are intentionally and unintentionally ignorant of the hurts and pain of the poor. The educated will not take the actions needed to help all children become better educated. Wars continue because we need to ensure an oil supply, even as people die. Power is part of the need … and the powerless remain powerless because they are not given voice.

Torture. Malnutrition. Starvation. Sexual, emotional, physical and spiritual abuse. The list is endless. Excuse the change of metaphor, but perhaps because the mountain is so high we will take not even the first steps upward to reach toward correcting the injustices.

For myself, I wish to try to correct and change the injustices that are perpetuated against lgbt persons. By doing a little, perhaps it will help move thoughtful people to use their gifts, skills, experiences and energies for correcting not only these injustices, but other problems as well.

Dr. Franklin H. Littell, a Methodist minister, college professor, Holocaust expert, scholar, and world citizen, was a frequent contributor to *Christian Ethics Today*. He wrote of Martin Niemoeller, one of the most respected Protestant leaders in Germany. After a signal career as a decorated U-Boat captain in the First World War, Niemoeller became a Christian advocate. In 1933, he was in charge of a prestigious suburban parish in Berlin-Dahlem, when he became the highest profile of Hitler's Christian opponents.

Niemoeller was a leader in the mobilization of the Pastors' Emergency League, the Synod that denounced the abuses of the dictatorship in the famous "Six Articles of Barmen." Other visible joint actions and sermons finally led to his arrest on 1 July 1937. There were then a few honest judges still functioning in Germany, and when the court let him go with a slap on the wrist, Hitler personally ordered his incarceration. Niemoeller was in a concentration camp, including long periods of solitary confinement, until the end of the war.

After the war, active in international church affairs, he made preaching trips across the United States. He brought the message of concern for others, often driving the point home with a confession of his own blindness when the Nazi regime first rose to power.

Niemoeller's message carried a powerful moral influence. He wrote:

> "First they came for the communists, and I did not speak out because I was not a communist. Then they came for the socialists, and I did not speak out because I was not a socialist. Then they came for the trade unionists, and I did not speak out because I was not a trade unionist. Then they came for the Jews, and I did not speak out because I was not a Jew. Then they came for me, and there was no one left to speak out."

What do I hope for?

Integrity. Openness. Honesty. Self-examination of conscience that leads to appropriate outward action. In other words, faith that is full of life and activity.

Two of my friends had jobs with one of our national agencies, and after they left their national denominational jobs, apologized to me. They were sorry that they did not speak out earlier about their support of lgbt persons. They said that their jobs kept them from doing it.

I recall a conversation with another national staff person who did not share his faith clearly and publicly because he felt that he could not let conservatives know his true theological and faith perspective. That was before he headed an agency and now he feels that he has to protect his agency and cannot or should not speak out about lgbt concerns.

As a former district executive, national staff person, and national executive, I cannot claim that I had the courage to speak out on controversial issues. Was I afraid of losing my job? Actually, I think that thought did not enter my mind as much as the under-the-skin fear that I would be rejected. I knew that I was gay. I was secretive about it. I was silent. I feared that others would know. I was not taught by my parents that homosexuals go to hell, but my culture and the church made it clear that such a subject and such a life was a humongous no-no! It was not a matter of don't ask, don't tell. It was, rather, "don't even acknowledge it to yourself." The key words in my earlier life were that homosexuality was "abnormal, criminal and sinful."

I was secluded and silent. And, yes, I now want those who are lesbian, gay, bisexual, or transgender, and those supportive or nearly supportive allies, to come out. That's how the injustice is dealt with. Integrity. Honesty. Openness. Transparency. Authenticity.

Elie Wiesel, in his acceptance speech for the 1986 Nobel Peace Prize said: "I swore never to be silent whenever human beings endure suffering and humiliation. We must take sides. Neutrality helps the oppressor, never the victim. Silence encourages the tormentor, never the tormented. Sometimes we must interfere."

Transparent Leadership

Katharine Jefferts Schori, the current Presiding Bishop of the Episcopal Church of the U.S.A. elected in 2006, noted:

> "I think courage is a central characteristic of leadership. If you're not willing to go into dangerous places, you have no business doing this work. ... I'm clear about this role involving the entire breadth of the Episcopal Church. But at some level, I don't think it's appropriate for me to disguise what my own theological understanding is. I'm someone who believes transparency is incredibly important. It's part of integrity."

Initially when I wrote this reflection the title was "Prophetic Leadership." In thinking about the meaning of 'prophetic' I realized that other words may be helpful. I am hopeful that persons in leadership will be transparent, open, and direct in sharing their core values. I am hoping for a more outspoken, articulated and even confrontational (not Brethren, surely?) approach to difficult issues of justice. Transparency, for me, connotes working from a center of authenticity and integrity.

I admit that I am strongly biased. I want our leaders to state their own faith and core values clearly and distinctly. I urge them to say it when what they believe does not coincide with Annual Conference statements or district or congregational decisions. How can we have honest dialogue unless there is a willingness to be clear about what we believe? For instance, I come from a bias that our leaders have been reluctant to speak out about their personal beliefs in regard to sexual orientation and concerns in the church about ordination, membership, leadership, and union services. I am sometimes cynical and believe that leaders do not speak out because of the economic impact it might have on the church or on themselves. There are, however, many other reasons: theological, philosophical, political, and pragmatic.

I believe that difficult issues can be reconciled only when the leaders are familiar with biblical, historical, and ethical points of view regarding sexual orientation, and then clearly articulate their own personal values and biases.

I believe that often gays and lesbians have been left isolated and disenfranchised because church leaders have not been willing to educate themselves, have denied the severity of the conflict, and have decided that it is their role to stand in the middle and facilitate rather than be clear and speak out about their own values. Church leaders are too often more comfortable talking about other groups of people, than sharing their own views from their own experiences and lives. True mediation and reconciliation are possible only when the leaders are in open and honest dialogue.

I believe, in the words of a friend, that "Leadership is *the* issue facing our society. We see it in every sector of our society, government, education, business, and religious institutions. It is a discouraging and dismal picture."

I believe that while it is true that leaders have the responsibility, even the obligation, to listen to and represent the whole church, it is also true that leaders have the responsibility to educate, lead the way, and identify their own values. Is it possible to do both?

I believe that many of our leaders understand their primary role as that of facilitating dialogue. In that role, they may have abdicated their responsibility to "speak the truth in love." Our leaders, in order to keep peace within the denomination, do not make clear their own personal and deeply held values, theology, or beliefs.

It is my observation that the more conservative leaders in the denomination understand their responsibility and role to be that of being prophetic. Certainly it is so on the issues of sexual orientation. Moderate to progressive leaders, on the other hand, tend to lean over backwards to be sure that all voices are heard. That position seems to exclude, however, their own profound and sincerely held convictions.

In your role as a leader, if a governing body approves a statement or position that is in conflict with your deeply held values, what is your responsibility as a leader and as a person of faith? What are your choices?

I have recognized, upon recalling my own history, that I did not, in my executive positions, always speak out of my convictions. Do you wish you could do more than you do but are not allowed to do so or are kept from speaking out? What compels you to speak out? What holds you back?

In July 2005, when the Church of the Brethren Annual Conference heard a report on the "Polity of the Conference and General Board," the delegates added an item to the list of purposes and functions of the General Board: to "provide leadership in prophetic social policy development for the denomination." Why was it necessary to put that in writing? What does that imply, not only for the board of directors of the denomination, but for others in positions of leadership? I wonder - is the role of leader as advocate not acceptable? No longer needed? I believe that it is needed now more than ever.

I wonder – do we think that the first and basic concern for the church is to grow in numbers? My United Church of Christ friend stated that during the 2005 General Synod debate on same-sex marriage, the UCC President at that time, John Thomas, responded to the critical voices that were afraid of what the resolution would do to UCC membership and local church loss. He said that that is not the issue. The issue is what is right in terms the teachings of Jesus and the tradition of the UCC on matters of human dignity, justice, and love of our neighbor.

There are major leadership needs and problems facing the Church of the Brethren. We must identify the foundation upon which we formulate the purposes and goals of leadership. We can work toward resolving the tension between what we believe to be right and true . . . and what we perceive the people in the church think and believe. We must affirm that we are all created by one God and Creator. That affirmation must be based on the premise of open and honest dialogue – dialogue that includes the forthcoming of our own deeply held convictions.

Schori stated: "I don't think it's appropriate for me to disguise what my own theological understanding is."

Audrey deCoursey, our associate pastor remarked: "This term, 'to disguise' is key: the distinction of transparent, authentic leadership is not using authority to indoctrinate but refusing to mislead and disguise."

Jesus as CEO

Did you know that Jesus learned, in his fourteen years of trying to develop a new organization, to always take a vote before proceeding? He discovered, for instance, that the Gathered Community needed to agree, with at least 80% approval before he was allowed to heal anyone.

They, as a new movement, did not want to upset the traditional Jewish community. They had seen what happened to those who were perceived as false prophets, and feared what would happen if folks decided that Jesus was one. In the past, such a rumor had split synagogues and sometimes families.

The Gathered Community did not want to upset the hierarchy. After all, the rabbinical counsel were the ones who decided how any action or activities of the GC would be interpreted. Ultimately, the rabbinical counsel approved any appointments to the rabbinical school. The official approval of the ministry of Jesus was, the community felt, hanging on a thread. There had been other leaders – even with rabbinic status – who had, through the action of the Counsel, lost their set-apart ministry role. Go up against the wrong folks in the province and you could lose your ordination.

Some of the members of the GC argued, "We should be particularly careful or they won't let us have a booth during the summer festival. We would not be allowed to sell our peace doves and monogrammed prayer shawls."

Also, Jesus and the disciples, despite their strong views, did not want to upset the secular community, those on the 'political right,' those politicians who also understood themselves to be both political and religious. Upsetting that group could bring about grave misunderstandings. The support of that group was needed because they were the ones who frequently made laws or developed restrictive statewide legislation that might affect the GC.

Don't upset the Gentiles because some of that group may want to follow Jesus. It's mighty poor evangelism to preach values that might cause others to turn away. Don't upset fellow Jews because the synagogue could split, or, as in the past, a new Jewish movement could start.

And as this new leader spoke out the very conservative Jews were not silent. "What you are doing is against the Law as we interpret it." And, "God has told us what the Law is." "We Jews were always persecuted. Just look at our history. Make the Romans mad and then see what will happen. They will tear down the temple. We will be sent to a foreign land. Stick to our historic religion – as we understand it. Don't be heretics. Don't get us in trouble."

So the Gathered Community developed a process. They elected a Board of Directors. The Board appointed committees. For instance, before Jesus could preach to the gatherings on the Mount of Olives, they had committees appointed to work on:

> plans for distributing the offering and gifts the people gave;
> developing an outreach program;
> dealing with the noisy children that the parents brought along;
> marketing their beliefs without offending the majority;
>> (they were wise enough to know that you can't make everyone happy but you can try)
> working with diversity (Jews, Gentiles, Romans);
> placating women who might want to take leadership roles; and
> attracting interested male Gentiles who were not circumcised
> (other than it only hurts for a little while).

Jesus was in his early 30's and wanted to move ahead but he was advised to go slow. Historians noted, later on, that there was one of his disciples who tried to get him to move even faster than he wanted to. That one came to a no-good end.

The followers who cautioned that he move slowly said that he had plenty of time. The man who lived healthily could expect to live at least into his early 50's. Jesus' health was good. He had yearly physicals. Jesus had plenty of time in his life. They advised, "What will be, will be!" "In God's own good time!" "Trust God – don't make waves."

The pressure was ever present. "Move slowly. Very slowly. Do not divide the synagogue. Do not divide the Jewish community. Do not upset Herod. Do not upset the Romans."

The organizational approach for the new movement included a vision and mission statement, time-limited objectives and yearly end-result evaluations. The GC lasted for many, many years. Jesus retired in his early forties in order to spend personal time with his family, and another rabbi was appointed to take his place. The GC had a booth at the annual festival, and was occasionally honored by the folks in charge of the festival. Unfortunately, other than what is written here, this is all that we know of the group known as "The Gathered Community."

Sleeping Through a Revolution

I know you inside and out, and find little to my liking. You're not cold, you're not hot—far better to be either cold or hot! You're stale. You're stagnant. You make me want to vomit. You brag, 'I'm rich, I've got it made, I need nothing from anyone,' oblivious that in fact you're a pitiful, blind beggar, threadbare and homeless.

Revelation 3:15-17 (The Message)

Martin Luther King, Jr. preached the last Sunday morning worship service of his life at the National Cathedral in Washington, D.C. It was the 31st of March, 1968, only five days before he was assassinated. The title of the sermon was "Remaining Awake through a Great Revolution." King began the sermon by reminding his hearers of Washington Irving's well-known story of "Rip Van Winkle," asserting that the most unique aspect of the story was not simply that Rip Van Winkle slept for twenty years. Of much more importance, during those twenty sleeping years, a revolution occurred. When Van Winkle went up into the mountain, King George III of England ruled the land in which he lived, but when Van Winkle came down twenty years later, George Washington was president of a new nation. Rip Van Winkle had slept through a revolution!

After reminding his hearers of the Rip Van Winkle story, Martin Luther King asserted that "one of the great liabilities of life is that all too many people find themselves living amid a great period of social change and yet they fail to develop new attitudes, the new mental responses that the new situation demands. They end up sleeping through a revolution." In King's mind, of course, it was the unfolding civil rights movement, challenging the fabric of racism at the core of our society, that all too many were missing. Even more, there was a human rights revolution literally exploding around the world, with all manner of persons standing up for freedom, justice, and peace. Proclaimed King in his sermon that Sunday morning, "Yes, we do live in a period where changes are taking place and there is still the voice crying through the vista of time saying, 'Behold, I make all things new, former things are passed away.'"

I wonder . . .

Are we lukewarm when it comes to issues of peace and justice?

Are we sleeping through a revolution?

Are the members and leaders in the church called to be revolutionary?

Are we called to be completely, utterly, and outrageously just?

Several friends have shared their thoughts in this regard: "We as Brethren do not wish to be outrageous ... unless it is safe. And then it is not outrageous, is it? It goes against our Brethrenism to be too adventurous when it comes to dealing with injustice."

"Are we, really, a justice-seeking people?"

"I guess we need others to be prophets and to lead the way because our work, our theology, and our beliefs do not allow us to be prophets."

I am reminded of an alleged conversation between Ralph Waldo Emerson and Henry Thoreau. Midway in his two-year Walden sojourn, Thoreau had spent a night in jail protesting the Mexican-American War, an event he reflected on in the famous and influential essay "Civil Disobedience" (1849). His friend Ralph Waldo Emerson came to visit him in jail and said to Thoreau "What are you doing in there?" and Thoreau responded; "What are you doing out there?"

It is my belief that the church and its leaders are *called* to model and lead out on issues of justice. It is horrendous that the church continues to deny support to persons who are lgbt. To speak out and influence the direction and the dialogue of the church – that is both prophetic and professional. This is the fortuitous moment in our nation and in our history to move from silence and personal support to open advocacy for justice on lgbt issues. The revolution is here . . . now.

Sitting on the fence is awkward. Now is the time to speak out. As noted recently by an observer of the current climate, "It is going to be ugly because the right wing is losing now, losing its hold on popularizing anti-gay attitudes. They will not go down without a fight."

For a congregation that maintains silence on justice it will become more difficult as the culture becomes more open. That is, in the years ahead it will be more difficult to be a bigoted congregation. Health care, colleges, universities, businesses, and industries are taking stands as they hire qualified lgbt persons. They are providing health care, normal benefits, and equal employment. They have people committed to moving ahead.

What holds us back? The writer of Revelation makes it all too clear: for we are neither hot nor cold. To be really inclusive is to be revolutionary ... and that is disquieting and disturbing in our very souls. We cannot, indeed, <u>must</u> not, sleep through this revolution.

The Times They Are A-Changin'

You recall that resounding Bob Dylan warning of 1963:

> Come gather 'round people wherever you roam
> And admit that the waters around you have grown
> And accept it that soon you'll be drenched to the bone.
> If your time to you is worth savin', then you better start
>   swimmin'
> Or you'll sink like a stone
> For the times they are a-changin'.

Change of some nature is inevitable. Sometimes the change is good, sometimes not so good. A new CEO takes the helm. Those in management development know, with certainty, that this will result in some change in the ranks: someone who does not like the new leader's style will leave; the new CEO will wish for certain persons to move into new positions. As a search consultant I would forewarn the staff of the agency hiring a new executive that there would be a trickle-down change as a result of the new executive management.

A change in a government's leadership will mean not only a change in cabinet positions, but sometimes, sadly, the loss of life as the new dictator promotes or encourages or ignores the genocide of an ethnic minority. A change in leadership may have a positive or negative effect on the human rights of those living in that country.

As a now retired Church of the Brethren professional (thirty years as a pastor, district executive, national staff and national executive, and then twelve years as a non-denominational hospice chaplain) I have witnessed changes within our denomination in regard to attitudes and actions pertaining to gays and lesbians.

As a married man who came out to family and friends in the 70's and 80's and more publicly in the 90's, my hope for change in the attitude of the church has been, of course, deeply personal. It was in the early 90's, during my yearlong CPE residency at Rush Presbyterian St. Luke's Medical Center in Chicago that I came to the grief-filled decision that I would no longer take a professional church position if I could not be open as a gay man. A few years later my thoughtful wife and I decided that 'in order to honor each other' we would separate.

Through all of these many years of consciousness about my sexual orientation, I kept a distant, yet intense watch on the attitudes and actions of the denomination.

In 1983 while I was an executive on the national staff, the Annual Conference of the Church of the Brethren approved its Human Sexuality Statement. While confirming human rights for all persons, the paper included a benchmark paragraph condemning and disallowing covenant relationships, namely between same gender persons. That one paragraph has become *the defining dogma.*

This statement has allowed the planning committee for every Annual Conference to keep the Brethren Mennonite Council for LGBT Interests from being fully involved in the Annual Conference. Most often it was not allowed to have a booth in the Exhibit Hall. Since 1983 it was allowed to have an official luncheon only a couple of times. It could not participate in the normal process of having Insight Sessions.

From time to time the planning committee for the Annual Conference showed more flexibility than at other times. In recent years, however, the Program and Arrangements Committee has been resolute and unmoving. BMC has been allowed no presence. Again it has been duly noted by the Program and Arrangements Committee that the reason for denial of visibility has been the statement on covenantal relationships in the 1983 Human Sexuality Statement.

Progressive leadership within the denomination has also used the 1983 Annual Conference Statement on Human Sexuality as legitimation and proof-texting for their less than progressive support.

I was often angered by the inaction of the leadership. My anger was often directed – not voiced - to the few who stated privately and in confidence, "I really do support you. I simply can't say anything publicly." Some of that is changing. Some retired professors and professionals are beginning to be public with their support of lgbt persons. One judicatory executive took the chance of losing his job and stated that while he has the responsibility to support the Annual Conference decisions, he, personally, recognized that the Human Sexuality decision about covenantal relationships was unjust. He is no longer in a District Executive position. Part of the pressure for him to move on may have been his willingness to clearly state his position.

Brethren Mennonite Council has progressed in great strides. It has become, in over 30 years of existence, more articulate, has many more active participants, a full-time executive and full-time volunteer, and a substantial budget. Other voices and organizations – albeit mostly not official ones – have supported and encouraged open and affirming action. The strong feminist Church of the Brethren Womaen's Caucus has become a powerful and outspoken ally. A more recent organization, Voices for an Open Spirit, joined in a chorus of affirmation not only for lgbt persons but also for *all* theological persuasions. There have been a number of national conferences, which even though they have not been primarily about lgbt issues, have not been encumbered with asking, "Who can be at the table of the Lord?"

Carol Wise, Executive Director of Brethren Mennonite Council for LGBT Interests, is somewhat optimistic about the future for lesbians, gays, bisexuals and transgender persons. In her comments at the end of 2006 she wrote; "Things are truly changing! I note that challenges to marriage equality are all but dead now in Canada. And in the US, I am hearing a subtle shift in the tone of the debate. Instead of careful calls for conversation and qualifying statements such as: "speaking just from my experience..." or "I understand this is a difficult issue..." I see more and more people naming a queer positive perspective as a matter of fact. For example, in a *Washington Post* editorial about Mary Cheney's pregnancy (Mary Cheney is usually simply referred to as "the Vice President's lesbian daughter"), moderate opinion writer Ruth Marcus notes 'the clanging disconnect between the Republican Party's outmoded intolerance and the benign reality of gay families today.'"

Notice what is happening in business and commerce as the country continues to move into the future. Read part of the following report from the Human Rights Campaign. It was written in 2007. Up-to-date information on ratings can be found at www.hrc.org.

WASHINGTON — The Human Rights Campaign today released a report showing that a record number of the largest U.S. companies are increasingly competing to expand benefits and protections for their gay, lesbian, bisexual and transgender employees and consumers. This year's report, the Human Rights Campaign's fifth annual Corporate Equality Index, showed an unprecedented 138 major U.S. companies earned the top rating of 100 percent. That number is up from 101 in 2005, and has grown tenfold in four years.

"I am incredibly encouraged and optimistic about the findings in this report. Companies are not only working to improve their scores, they are actively competing to be ranked the most inclusive and fair-minded in their industry," said Human Rights Campaign President Joe Solmonese. "Leading companies, which years ago instituted basic equal employment policies, are accelerating their efforts to expand the range of benefits. This competition sends a clear message that corporate America is rapidly becoming a place of fairness for GLBT Americans."

"CEOs are very much aware of their score and its impact on their business. They know that a top score means a healthier work environment, greater productivity and the ability to recruit top talent. They also know that a bad score will hurt their bottom line," Solmonese added.

"Corporations are rapidly adopting a more complete vision of fairness for GLBT employees in policy and practice," said Daryl Herrschaft, director for HRC's Workplace Project and author of the report. "These findings reflect a common desire in organizations today to move at a heightened pace to implement fair and equal policies for GLBT employees and then work to publicize their achievements."

And nations - yes, nations – have approved same-sex marriages. In 2007, same-sex marriages are recognized in Belgium, Canada, the

Netherlands, South Africa, and in Spain. Now, in 2009, in the United States same-sex marriages are currently legal in six states: Connecticut, Iowa, New Hampshire, Vermont, Maine and Massachusetts. As of 2007 civil unions, domestic partnerships or registered partnerships offer varying amounts of the benefits of marriage and are available in: Andorra, Croatia, Czech Republic, Denmark, Finland, France, Germany, Iceland, Israel, Luxembourg, New Zealand, Norway, Portugal, Slovenia, Sweden, Switzerland and the United Kingdom. They are also available in parts of Argentina, Brazil, Italy, Mexico, all Australian states and territories, the U.S. states of Connecticut, Hawaii, Maine, New Jersey, and the U.S. District of Columbia (Washington, DC).

In the United States, denominations are dissimilar on lgbt issues. Some of the denominations approving ordination and union services for gays and lesbians include the United Church of Christ, Episcopal Church USA, Friends (via meeting approval), Evangelical Lutheran Church of America, the Unitarian-Universalist Association, and Metropolitan Community Church. Many of the denominations, as you know, are in intense open debate on the issues. Within certain denominations, latitude is given both to judicatories and to congregations. This is primarily in the area of being open and affirming. Usually the latitude does yet not pertain to ordination or celebration of unions.

The Episcopal Church has ordained Gene Robinson as Bishop of New Hampshire in August 2003, the first open gay man elected as a bishop in the Episcopal Church. And they elected a woman, Katharine Jefferts Schori, the new Primate of the Episcopal Church. Schori, as senior bishop, encourages the church to be inclusive. Bishop John Shelby Spong wrote on July 5, 2006, "Katharine Jefferts Schori is a symbol that the world does change. Prejudice and stereotypes do die. The drive toward sexual equality and full humanity for all people does succeed. It is exhilarating to recognize that the pain that must always be endured in order to break down prejudices is worth it."

I have wondered why the Church of the Brethren, which, in my perspective, was ahead of others when it came to abolition of slavery and more recent civil rights concerns, which has stood with only a few others during wartime to advocate peace, and which strongly believes (sometimes not strongly enough) in the rights of women when it comes to abortion, ordination and the place of women in leadership ...... why does this denomination take a back seat when it comes to this issue of justice for gays and lesbians? Where is the biblical and theological advocacy for this particular justice issue?

While the preceding paragraph is negative, I think that we as a denomination are making some progress, albeit slowly. There are now twenty-four large and small congregations in our denomination that are publicly open and affirming, and another dozen or more that are in serious conversation about what it would mean to be publicly inclusive.

The times are truly changing. For moral, ethical, biblical, and theological reasons the denominations must recognize that they must support this national and international change for justice for lgbt persons.

"The real voyage of discovery consists not in seeking new landscapes, but in having new eyes."   Marcel Proust

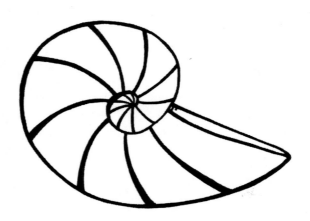

Aging and Saging

Aging

One cannot do anything about aging. As I heard countless times during hospice work, "Aging is better than the alternative."

I suppose most of us could say a lot about our aging – at any age:

That, for instance, we should take better care of our health;

That we should have a positive attitude about living and enjoy the life that we have;

That we should not let the past be a burden, live vigorously in the present, but look forward to the future.

I do not need to give much space here to "aging." There are countless, endless, and often useless articles on aging in books, magazines, and the ever-present Internet.

There is one set of aging statistics, however, that may be overlooked.

Whether you love them or have persistent misgivings, the baby boomer generation has profoundly changed the landscape of the United States and Canada. The Stonewall Rebellion in 1969 heralded a new era in civil rights for lgbt persons and began a significant shift in the understanding of human sexuality.

Lgbt people who grew up in a pre-Stonewall era were shaped by a life experience where their desires and their lives were characterized as criminal, mentally ill, evil and abnormal. The risks and the courage that so many exhibited in spite of the tremendous consequences is often stunning to consider. Yet for many, the scars remain.

It is estimated that there are approximately 2.9 million gay and lesbian people in the US who are over the age of 65. Research indicates that, in contrast to the larger community, elder gay and lesbian people are at high risk for isolation. Such research does not exist for bisexual and transgender elders. They are less likely to have a contact in time of crisis, more likely to live alone, more likely to have no life partner, more likely to have no children, and more likely to experience depression, poverty and illness.

They are also more reluctant to access social services. Most feel a need to return to the closet in order to access services safely. Elder lgbt persons face ongoing discrimination as they are shunned by the lgbt community because of age, shunned by the general population because of heterosexism, and denied basic rights related to hospital visitation by a partner.

Elder lgbt persons face unique financial challenges. Social Security survivor and/or spousal benefits are not available. Medicaid regulations protect the assets and homes of married spouses when the other spouse enters a nursing home; no such protections are offered to same-sex partners. There is discrimination in pension and 401(k) laws. Living partners often are handicapped in the provisions of inheritance laws.

A hostile social environment has meant that many of us as lgbt people have created our own families of choice and uniquely relied upon our own communities for survival. In this sense, lgbt elders are leading the way in terms of what many non-lgbt people are now beginning to experience due to numerous changes in family structures and lifestyles. Yet we as a community are challenged to do better than we have done in terms of advocating and caring for the elder lgbt people among us.[4]

The Brethren Mennonite Council for LGBT Interests has initiated an Elder LGBT Task Force to educate the broader community and address the needs of BMC elders to:

> Raise the visibility of lgbt elders within the BMC community
> Offer opportunities for gathering and connection
> Assess the lgbt friendliness of Mennonite and Brethren retirement communities
> Advocate for lgbt-positive policies and practices at Mennonite and Brethren retirement communities, including staff sensitivity training

---

4   National Gay and Lesbian Task Force website

Provide information and resources as needed by the elder Brethren and Mennonite lgbt community.

It is an excellent concept and a major challenge to try to develop an outreach program with all of our older communities. That includes the recognition of lgbt elders.

Saging

My friend, Martha Bartholomew, has encouraged me to understand that a complementary term to go along with aging is 'saging.'

Aging does not guarantee saging or wisdom. A lot of older people are not particularly wise. In fact, they are often similar to how they were as younger adults: naïve and opinionated. A sage is a person that learns and is open to an uncertain future. A sage, in development terms, embraces the nuances of life, realizing that his or her life is not endless.

I recall in hospice work the number of times that the staff ran up against a patient who was cantankerous, out of sync with life in general, and non-compliant with medicinal treatment. The general consensus was that just because Sam was now facing the end of his life did not mean that suddenly he would become a loving, gentle, forgiving, and wise person, now able to deal graciously with dying with dignity. No way. Generally, the attitudes developed and learned through life simply continued into illness and dying.

As an older adult I claim both aging and saging. Or at least I claim some of the saging.

What are some of the characteristics of a so-called 'sage?' What is wisdom and how does it come about?

David, the psalmist, was a sage, for he understood the depth of living.

O Lord, you have searched me and you know me.
You know when I sit and when I rise:
You perceive my thoughts from afar.
You discern my going out and my lying down;
  you are familiar with all my ways.
Before a word is on my tongue you know it completely,
  O Lord.
You hem me in – behind and before;
  you have laid your hand upon me.

Such knowledge is too wonderful for me, too lofty for me
to attain.

Psalm 139

The writer of the Old Testament Book of Proverbs may be considered a sage.

> To know wisdom, and instruction; to understand the words of prudence: and to receive the instruction of doctrine, justice, and judgment, and equity; to give subtlety to little ones, to the young man knowledge and understanding. A wise man shall hear and shall be wiser: and he that understandeth, shall possess governments. He shall understand a parable, and the interpretation, the words of the wise, and their mysterious sayings. The fear of the Lord is the beginning of wisdom. Fools despise wisdom and instruction. Prov.1:1-17

I do claim saging to some degree. Probably a real sage has one characteristic I seem to be denying: humility. Regardless, I wish to claim at least a little of being a sage.

+ Being degraded and disenfranchised as a human has led me *to be more sensitive to those who are in pain.*

+ Being a hospice chaplain working with dying gay men infected with AIDS, I learned a lot about the hostility and fear of family, friends and Christians. *In time, I learned something of the shadow side of humans.*

+ I respect and accept the *valiant struggles and courage of those who have gone before me.* I am thankful for those who have blazed the trail, who have forged ahead when the path was unknown. The foreparents of our lgbt 'family' who took decisive steps and, with courage, 'came out' when it might have been dangerous to do so. They are my teachers and mentors.

+ I know that *I am not alone* in this world. Yes, sometimes I feel that I am. But if I am willing I can let others know of my 'aloneness' and I can, in the lgbt and straight communities, find support and caring, if I am persistent enough. There are caring, forgiving and loving friends and family. Sometimes this community of family and friends must be given time. After all, how long has it taken me to understand and accept myself? And I am still in that search process.

+ Part of Buddhist belief is to understand that I cannot redo the past, nor can I predict the future: *What I have is the present. Now.* Living in the 'present only' space is sometimes very difficult. It saves a lot of energy and worry if one can accept 'what is' rather than 'what I wish it would be.'

+ Standing with that concept is another equally powerful Buddhist idea: that sorrow, tragedy, illness and joy, prosperity, and health are *the givens of living*. Our Christian God, given so many anthropomorphic attributes, is not a harsh and unforgiving dictator nor a benevolent, manipulative gift giver, favoring some and slapping down others. I am not lucky, or favored, or threatened, or any one of hundreds of other adjectives that attribute uncertain or uncaring actions to this sometimes indescribable god.

+ In terms of aging, and growing older, it is possible, if one wishes, to have an *overview of life*. Eric Erikson describes life's developmental levels. "Late Adulthood" is the time of 65 until death. The developmental outcomes of this level include integrity over against despair. The basic strength is *wisdom*.

> Erikson felt that much of life is preparing for the middle adulthood stage and the last stage is recovering from it. Perhaps that is because as older adults we can often look back on our lives with happiness and contentedness, feeling fulfilled with a deep sense that life has meaning and we've made a contribution to life, a feeling Erikson calls integrity. Our strength comes from a wisdom that the world is very large and we now have a detached concern for the whole of life, accepting death as the completion of life.

> On the other hand, some adults may reach this stage and despair at their experiences and perceived failures. They may fear death as they struggle to find a purpose to their lives, wondering "Was the trip worth it?" Alternatively, they may feel they have all the answers (not unlike going back to adolescence) and end with a strong dogmatism that only their view has been correct.[5]

---

5   Arlene F. Harder, MA, MFT, "The Developmental Stages of Erik Erikson," © Copyright 2002, Revised 2009,   LearningPlacesOnLine.com

Life is a journey, isn't it? Despite the occasional despair, I am glad that my life has been full.

> How precious to me are your thoughts, O God!
> How vast is the sum of them.
> Were I to count them, they would outnumber the
> grains of sand.
> When I awake, I am still with you.

From Psalm 139

A Story about Chagrin

Someplace along the line in my budding professional career as a pastor, I had learned that I did not like the stereotypic images that people had of ministers.

I often laughed – perhaps cringed – at the story about the minister who went skinny dipping in the YMCA pool. (Years ago that was not unusual.) Another man – someone the minister did not know and had not seen before - came into the pool area, saw the very naked minister treading water, and said "Good morning, Reverend."

Certain stereotypes came about because – well, because they grew up out of truths. But I didn't like it. I wanted to be atypical. And I kept an eye out for ways to avoid being 'put in a box.'

One such opportunity came in the summer of 1966. For weeks I had been on the road campaigning in my bid for the congressional seat for the Second District of Indiana. Yes, running for office. I had been a pastor at the Lafayette Church of the Brethren for 8 years and had become involved with politics in the city and in the Second District. How that happened is another story.

Winning the primary and going into the general election had been quite enlightening. I was on a 'leave of absence' with the blessings of the congregation. In fact, one of the church board members had said, when granting the leave, "Now you can practice what you preach." Or perhaps he meant, "It's about time that you practice what you preach."

In my campaign I had been very cautious about 'preaching.' I did not think it was a good idea to be seen as a minister. I thought, "Too many stereotypes of ministers. I want to run this campaign as a citizen, not as a minister." And my campaign committee agreed.

On this particular occasion I was to speak to the Women's Democratic Club of White County. It was an evening affair with a 7:00 p.m. presentation, followed by an informal reception.

I had been explicit when talking with the woman who would introduce me. "Lucille," I implored, "I prefer to be introduced, simply, as Ralph McFadden, seeking a public office on behalf of the people of Second District."

I was, therefore, momentarily chagrined - perhaps even stunned - when Lucille, also the president of the Club, with great enthusiasm and eloquence and a radiant smile, introduced me as "Ralph McFadden, our minister from Lafayette, Indiana." Applause, applause!

Hmmm? Should I say anything? No, guess not. I went ahead with the presentation without commenting on the introduction. I could forgive Lucille. In her more rural upbringing, it probably made sense that a minister was highly respected, or at least more respected than a politician.

I thought the speech went very well. I can be enthusiastic and forthright, even if I may not be saying much. The audience was attentive, laughed at the humor, nodded seriously on the issues, and applauded enthusiastically.

Then I was escorted over to the cookies and coffee area, where a white linen tablecloth covered the usual 3 by 8-foot collapsible table. I was introduced to different supporters as they came through the line to greet "their candidate."

And then came a second moment for chagrin – and later reflection on the nature of my ministerial calling. A woman, probably in her sixties, with lovely white hair, make-up subtle and understated, came up beside me, took my left elbow in her right hand, reached across and patted me on the chest with her left hand, and speaking with assurance and clarity said, "Ralph, that didn't sound like a minister at all. That sounded like you knew what you were talking about!"

Fated to return to the professional ministry if I lost the bid for office, I almost wish I had won that election.

The Kid and Work

I remember Troy, Ohio. For a lot of reasons.

It was a 'growing up' time in my life. My family lived in Troy from the time I was in fourth grade until the end of my eleventh grade.

I helped mow the grass, a push mower. It seemed like it was at least five acres, though it was, I think, closer to half an acre. We also truck gardened. Over the years we were in Troy, Dad and Mom raised soybeans, tomatoes and popcorn.

I remember each of those products. 1500 tomato plants. Many were planted – sort of a gamble – as early in the season as possible so that Dad would be one of the first truck-farmers to get his produce into the grocery stores. Dad and Mom picked the tomatoes, polished each one, and carefully laid them in the small woven baskets, red and juicy bottom side up, all the better to sell. The grocers in Troy looked forward to Dad bringing in the produce. For us kids all the weeds had to be hoed, and the rows cultivated. For years we three brothers, in unison, could say, "I hate stewed tomatoes." And the smell! Ugh! It would get on your bib overalls, and shoes, and on your hands. I sure can recognize that smell.

The soybeans were quite a different product and we probably only raised them a year or two. When the bean plants got old and brown, then it was time to harvest. And the edges of the bean shells were tough, brittle and sharp. We wore gloves to harvest the beans. Then the shells had to be broken open, and the little soybeans shelled. I don't recall what Dad and Mom did with them. Somebody probably bought them to make soup.

Raising popcorn wasn't half bad. Yes, there was the hoeing and cultivating. And finally, in the fall, when the corn stocks had turned brown, we hand-harvested the ears, one at a time, then took the leaves off of the corn cobs. Later, in the fall, we would sit in the living room, listening to "The Lone Ranger Rides Again" and shelling the corn. The easiest way to shell popcorn was to rub one ear of corn against another, let the shelled corn fall into a bucket. I remember we raised a white popcorn called "Japanese Hulless." When the kernels of that corn were popped, they had no ugly brown hulls. During the Second World War, someone changed the name of the popcorn from Japanese Hulless to Australian Hulless. Hmmm!

But that was work at home. Many were the years that each of us as brothers also worked away from home. My years of child labor included a paper route, taking up a route that older brother Bob and then Wilbur had. My first year with newspapers, however, was when I was in fifth grade and I sold – hawked – the Troy Daily News at the Waco Glider company. That was in about 1944, during the war. I was eleven. I would go to the employee exit of the Waco Glider plant, and then, as one crew left work and another came to work, I would stand there, newspapers in hand, and shout "Newspaper! Get your Troy Daily News!" The paper was four cents, but sometimes they would give me a nickel. That was a penny tip. That was okay!

After the paper route I worked in a shoe store. That was right before I worked in Brower's Stationery Store. Bob and Wilbur had also worked in Brower's, but the shoe store was all mine. I was not following an older brother. That was an unusual experience. The owner was – to me – an old man. I remember the cigars he smoked and the smell. I think, because of Mr. Spinoza, I still hate cigars, especially the smell.

At the time I began to work for The Troy Shoe Store – now that was a unique name! – I was a freshman in high school. I think I lasted a year. I can still see that store, the two rows of chairs, women's shoes on one side of the store and men's on the other. The children's shoes were at the back. The rows of chairs were two sided, each row was a combined set of chairs with their backs to each other. Spaced here and there in the aisles were mirrors on the floor, so that the customer could admire his or her feet in the new shoes.

Old man Spinoza gave his employees special training. For instance, I earned a dollar if I sold a pair of shoes that he was trying to get rid of. "When showing shoes to the customer, be sure to offer to the men that special black wing tip, and if you sell it, you get a dollar extra in your pay." Not a paycheck. No checks. Cash.

And Spinoza was sly as a fox. He taught me, and I still don't know if it's true, that just before you put the shoe on the customer's foot, give the instep of the foot a nice friendly squeeze, a snug squeeze, and then the shoe, even if it is not a perfect fit, will feel like a good fit. Sneaky, huh?

So the big deal was to sell them a shoe they may not want so that I could earn an extra dollar, and one that did not exactly fit, because I squeezed their foot.

One other thing I learned from the owner: every once in a while he would take me over to Brumbaugh's Restaurant, and buy dessert. He left Hazel in the store. She could take care of things. Cigar smoking Spinoza would buy me a slice of apple pie, and always order his apple pie with a slice of cheese on top of it. He would, with a twinkle in his eye, "Apple pie without its cheese is like a kiss without a squeeze."

I still like apple pie, with a crust on the top and on the bottom, and a slice of sharp cheddar cheese.

Later on, four years to be exact, when I was a freshman in college and home for the summer, I landed a job in JC Penney's selling guess what? - shoes. I still gave the customer a friendly, foot squeeze before putting a shoe on.

A Tale of Two

It was early morning. It was still dark. I could hear, as always, the waterfall as it flowed over the protruding rocks and drained into the fishpond in our back yard. I was fully awake and I thought as I lay there, "I am content."

Content! That's a great word. At peace with myself and the circumstances in which I found myself. Satisfied and happy with the relationship with Keo. Glad for our home, my occasional work, and our health. It has taken a long time to come from the seclusion of the closet to openness – and contentedness.

I am content . . . yet wanting the church to continue to change. I am not desperate and no longer naïve. I am trying to understand why people are so homophobic and fearful, still trying to understand the fear of homosexuality or just sexuality issues, and trying to understand the faith-based, theological and biblically based hostility. I admit I am not trying very hard for I also confess that I have little respect for those who have those deeply held biblically-based and personally-based biases against lgbt persons.

Content . . . and even though I do not understand the depth of hostility, fear, and misunderstanding, I acknowledge that fundamentalism is a fact of life for some people. I think they may be afraid to be open to a new way of understanding sexuality. I recall Carl, a college friend. He was a fundamentalist, and my suspicion was that if even one brick was pulled from his very solid belief wall, his whole understanding of faith and God would collapse.

Content . . . for I know that there are life-giving and life-fulfilling changes.

That's what this commentary is about. For the fact is that Joshua and Aaron, despite their fundamentalist backgrounds, are moving toward being

57

or have found that they are content. They have changed, and changed radically.

Both Aaron and Joshua, at different times, were referred to me by someone who thought that I might, as a gay man and a Christian, be a friend who could travel with them on this precarious journey of self-discovery.

Aaron, African American, was a graduate of Grinnell College, a small liberal arts school in Iowa, and the progressive Chicago Theological Seminary. He was the part-time Youth Pastor of an African American Baptist Church in the Chicago area. With the exception of a couple of liberal European-American friends in that congregation, folks did not know that he identified as gay.

In that church, he needed to silently put up with the periodic preaching pronouncements of the pastor and various ministers, that being a homosexual was a deviant and grievous sin.

Aaron was trying to find a meaning for his life. "Is it possible that God can change me into a straight person? Is it possible that I could find a woman I would marry and we could have children? I would love to have a family. What can I do with this terrifying reality that I am attracted to men and that I am condemned to hell if I cannot change that reality? Why does the church persecute me and others? Should I be confiding in the pastor? Would I lose my position as a youth minister if I did confide in the pastor or others? Is it possible that the pastor or the church would accept me as I am? Would the church demand that I repent – and promise never to be in a male relationship again?"

Aaron continued to search for direction. "I feel that I am called to ministry, but I can't see how that can be possible if I accept that I am gay. Will it be possible for me to find a career in ministry? I don't understand why God has put me in this position. What does God expect of me now? Am I loved by God as I am – or only if I change? What is my future? Can I be in the church? What are the options for my life?"

Joshua, a white, male young adult, has a similar and yet very different background. Joshua has grown-up in a conservative Protestant church all of his life. His parents are deeply involved with a conservative, fundamentalist congregation. Joshua's brother is a minister in that congregation. The church teaches and preaches that homosexuality is a perversion and an abomination against God.

Joshua's family knows that he is wrestling – really struggling – with his self-identity of being gay. Joshua has been taught by church, family and friends that being gay is simply not a Christian alternative.

He has questioned, "Are my desires simply the result of a deep inner conflict, such as not receiving enough attention from my father? Can the poor decisions I've made such as hooking up with men and browsing pornography be attributed to my homosexuality or are they a natural consequence of feeling defeated from the start? If my family had accepted me and engaged my relationships, would I have hidden in the dark? If the expectation for monogamy and sex within marriage existed for gays would I have made healthier choices? Am I a narcissist for thinking that God even cares about who I'm attracted to?"

He wondered, "How do I move out of this deep pit of self-absorption with being gay? Can I move out of it? I know that my family prays for me believing that God can change me. Why do I keep going to those downtown Chicago adult book stores? I am not happy with my life, but I see no path out of this storm of self-hatred."

Joshua and Aaron felt that their families and the church could not and never would believe that being gay was a justifiable option for anyone, let alone a Christian.

And now we can fast forward to the present. Aaron and Joshua, over months and years, have each moved forward and continue to move toward self-acceptance. "I am gay. And that's okay."

What has brought about the change for these two men?

Faced with the possibility of hell and damnation from their families, teachers, and preachers and having been taught beyond doubt that they were in the wrong - deadly in the wrong - survival demanded a change in attitude, behavior, outlook and self-confidence. Survival. Given the significant percent of suicides of lgbt persons, Aaron and Joshua have survived. They chose survival over going more deeply into the closet, and over taking their own lives.

Courage. Aaron ultimately made a decision to move back home to Texas to be with his mom and sisters who had come to accept his sexuality. He made the painful decision to leave that part-time ministry in an African-American church and seek membership in a largely European-American, liberal Baptist congregation. He was later ordained in the new church. They knew that he was gay and celebrated it with him. He also elected to do ministry in a hospital rather than in a congregation. In the last few months, he came out to his older brother, whom he feared would reject him. His brother, while somewhat concerned about Aaron's ultimate salvation, affirmed his personhood and affirmed his love for Aaron regardless of sexual orientation.

Joshua has moved out of his family home into Chicago. He still maintains a solid connection with his family, but his courage has given him the drive to seek out his life on his own.

Aaron added this acknowledgment: "Grace. This is unmerited love and affirmation from God, embodied in my friends. I have come out to a number of friends, mentors and even past teachers. All of whom have expressed their support for me."

Also, from my perspective in this tale of two, Aaron and Joshua have individual characteristics that have helped to pull them through: intelligence, thoughtfulness, insight, and awareness of changing attitudes in the culture. In addition, the passage of time, along with the acceptance of their own sexual reality, has made a difference.

I have wondered, as a friend, "What can a listener and counselor contribute to a movement toward wholeness for lgbt persons? What can a member of a church contribute toward this journey of self-discovery? Or, coming from a negative position, what does a member of a church do that discourages self-authentication?"

The listener and counselor must become more educated about the cultural and religious issues that are a part of the fabric of our society.

The listener must understand how homophobia damages the lgbt person.

The listener needs to see the central humanness of the person . . . the wholeness and not just the sexual component.

The listener must listen, learn, and subject him or herself to an open and even selfless awareness that could, ironically, be painful for the listener.

Content . . . Perhaps that is now a possible word to describe the journey for Aaron and Joshua. Not finished with the journey, but well on the road to self-discovery and self-acceptance.

A Letter to Jeremy

Dear Jeremy,

Last month you shared with us as a BMC board, that because of your doubts about God and your experience with an abusive church, you wondered about the ethics of staying on the board, an agency related to the church.

I thank you, Jeremy, for initiating the conversation. Your openness reminded me of an incident a number of years ago. I can still visualize the circumstances.

Barbara and I had separated in 1994. I was living in Denver and was staying, temporarily, in a 10th floor condo of a good friend. The condo had a balcony that faced the west. I could sit on the balcony and take in the beauty and majesty of the Colorado Rockies. I loved it.

It was August of 1995. A couple was visiting me – Blaine, 25 years old, and his fiancée, Diane, a seminary graduate. I had known Blaine about for several years. Loved that guy. And I deeply respected and loved Diane.

On that balcony one afternoon I came out to Blaine and Diane. Not as a gay man. They knew that. I came out about my faith, what I believed. It was not easy to do. In fact, I felt that perhaps it was more difficult sharing my faltering and changing faith than it had been to come out as gay. At that time I was not very clear but I knew that I had to let some friends know what I was thinking.

That's why I appreciate your courage. I assume that sharing this particular journey has been for you somewhat risky. Perhaps it is, in some ways, more difficult than coming out as lesbian, and then as transgender. I am a seminary graduate, have been a pastor and church executive, and a hospice chaplain. Expressing doubt about God did not fit what people expected of me.

Briefly, I do not put much emphasis on "believing" in a god. In some ways I really don't care. When I was in hospice work as a chaplain it was my responsibility to try to understand the faith perspective of the patient and family, take their understanding of faith seriously, and respond accordingly. Sometimes that was difficult. For the first five or so years of the 1990's I worked primarily with gay men with AIDS. I presided over memorial services and buried over 100 of those young men. Sometimes the patient had a longing for an assurance that God did not hate them. I could assure them that if God existed, then that God was a loving and totally forgiving God. Sometimes the family would reject the son. I then had the opportunity to work with the gay patient with AIDS – and his distraught family - hoping to reconcile them. That did not always work out. Callous as it may seem for me to say, I would pray with the patient and the family even though I did not believe as they believed. But the purpose of my counseling and prayer was simply to encourage and strengthen the person as he was dying.

I like the verse of a hymn that reads; "Prayer is the soul's sincere desire, uttered or unexpressed." My sincere desire, describe it as you will, was a prayer for self-acceptance for the patient, and openness on the part of the family and friends. That hymn verse still describes the way I understand prayer.

Sometimes I have had very little regard for the institutional church. I concur with you. The church is often toxic. It damages the life and soul of countless numbers of children, youth and adults.

Why then do I continue with involvement, for instance, in my local church? For a number of years in Denver and after I returned to Elgin, I intentionally attended no church. Then my grandniece was baptized and she asked me to attend. I did. I started to get re-involved. My intention then, as it is now, was not to find a place to worship God. I have had many years of re-interpreting the hymns and scriptures and religious language to suit my own understandings and my own life journey. My intention was to continue a faith journey that included family, friends and a community of persons who wanted to change the injustices of the world.

In regard to the institutional church, I am ambivalent. I guess my primary reason for attending and participating has been (1) to be with family and friends, (2) to try to encourage more openness and inclusiveness on the part of the congregation, and (3) to politically influence the denomination. The Church of the Brethren national offices are in Elgin. I worked there for over 18 years, and many of the national staff are my friends. I have had some influence, but I realize that there is still much to do. Perhaps being friends with someone when I have had a hidden agenda of trying to bring about lgbt education on concerns may not be ethical.

I have had some positive and negative experiences with the congregation and the denomination. But despite the negative experiences, I have stayed attached even though I have often fantasized about leaving. It somehow nourishes my Soul to know that I can be independent enough to leave (sometimes you can read that as 'flee'), if I wish.

I am glad, at least for now, that I have stayed very much in touch with the congregation. As you know I was dangerously ill this past summer (2008). I am thankful for the strength of the relationships of family and friends. Yes, many had me in their prayers. I know that some of them would be disappointed if I said that I valued their cards, phone calls, and personal support and visits more than their prayers. For me the calls, cards and visits were their prayers in action. I was very fortunate to have the support of family and friends. My two adult children were extremely supportive.

It is clear that I am willing to take living more seriously with the time that I have yet to live. One resolution is that I will try to connect with my family and friends with a deepening relationship. Another resolve is that I will try to support others who are going through grief, loss, sickness, and so forth. I think it is okay to realize that I am wiser than I was. I am on a journey, Jeremy. And so are you.

I encourage you to keep yourself open and courageous: to the experiences of the past, the moments of opportunity in the present, and the promises of the future.

Shalom,
Ralph

A Letter to Anne and Ken

Dear Anne and Ken,

Your call, Anne, has given me the opportunity to be reflective. I am very grateful that you trusted me and shared part of your life with me. I care deeply for each of you. I wish and hope that the two of you will have fulfilling lives. Your sharing, Anne, that you are likely bisexual, once again keeps me aware of the silent lives of countless men and women who are on journeys that family or friends may not understand.

When I was young, I knew that I had an attraction for boys of my age. But I had no idea that it would, one day, lead to such a journey and to such changes over a life span.

In my younger boyhood days I had sexual experiences/experimentation with other boys in junior high school. By the time I got into high school, college and graduate school, the sexual contact with males was over. I had fantasies, but did not have sexual involvement with men until after Barbara and I were no longer living together.

When I was a senior in high school my family moved to Elgin. My dad became the pastor of the Highland Avenue Church of the Brethren. Barbara, my wife to be, was a sophomore in high school. I had not dated before we moved to Elgin, so Barbara was my first dating experience. And though there was a brief time we were not together in college, we eventually married.

Perhaps I shared this with you in the past. In 1955, "getting married" was the thing to do. I grew up at a time when I had no models of what it might be to be a single gay man. 'Gay' was not in the vocabulary. 'Queer' and 'faggot' were the terms used. They were not kind words.

I did not consider staying single. It was expected that young men and women would, if possible, marry. So, during Barbara's sophomore year in college and my senior year, (both of us at Manchester College) we were engaged, had an engagement party, planned our wedding, sent out wedding invitations, and then, with approval of friends and family, committed ourselves to each other.

I remember the honeymoon. We went to a cottage on a lake in Michigan. I was not happy. I went outdoors at one point and cried. I did not know what I had gotten into. The sexual experience was not passionate. In time, because I was a young, virile man and because I wanted to be sexual, I found ways to have good sex and found ways, I think, for Barbara to enjoy it, too.

We had our first child, Joel, when I was a middler in seminary. 1959. We had our second child, Jill, the first year of our first major pastorate. All rejoiced over the birth of the two children. And I am delighted that we had them. I love them without reserve.

I do not regret our marriage. I have many, very good memories of it: life together, traveling, family vacations, family holidays, celebrating birthdays, school events, sports events, and having time with friends as we camped or cooked out.

We were thought of as an 'ideal family;' a married couple and two children – boy and girl. Later I would laugh about this: the father was gay, the son had a live-in girlfriend, and the daughter was lesbian. We did not fit the ideal pattern.

It was in the late 60's that I finally told Barbara that I was gay. Perhaps I said 'bisexual.' At that time in my history and in the language of homosexuals, 'gay' was hardly in. Homo, bisexual, heterosexual - I think those were the terms. I told Barbara about my sexual feelings because she was having a difficult time accepting my relationship to a woman I was close to. Barbara was likely correct in recognizing that that woman was interested in me. But I had no interest whatsoever. However, to calm the storm, I admitted and confessed that I was bi-sexual and that I was not interested in that woman. Notably, I did not say that I was not interested in any women. That likely would have dissolved our marriage very soon.

Over the following years we had to do a lot of talking. We agreed to stay married. We considered that, after all, we got along very well, enjoyed each other's company, and enjoyed many of the same things.

In the intervening years, many changes occurred in my thinking and in Barbara's. My own personal coming out to myself took time. But, within that time span, it became evident that I preferred men. I enjoyed their company and friendship. I was sexually attracted to different men.

My sexual activity with Barbara changed, so that in the last years of our marriage we simply were not sexual.

While we were in Denver, and as I became more public with my gay preferences, we finally decided that "in order to honor ourselves" we would separate. My regret now, as I look back, is that I did not take the initiative to separate earlier. It would have helped me to better define my own life choices, and it would have taken pressure off of Barbara to have to cover for me – and for her. I feel certain that as I and we came out to family and friends, their underlying questions had to do with why Barbara put up with the situation. Or why I did not have the courage or sense to move on with my life. At the time, before we made the divorce decision, we were often in conversation. We continued, during those conversations, to reaffirm that for us it seemed best and okay to continue to be married. But, eventually, we simply decided that the time had come to go our separate ways.

It is of interest to me how married couples, over time, come to many different conclusions about what to do with their sexual orientation differences.

- Maxwell, my age, decided to go the route of divorce. His wife had not been aware of his preferences. She was devastated and very angry.
- A divorced gay friend, Kyle, has said that he regrets that he got married. They had children. And when the children were teenagers Kyle and his wife divorced. Kyle, I think, wishes that he would have found a partner early in his adult life.
- A couple here in the Midwest has decided to stay together. They are retired - - and I do not think that will change.
- A pastoral couple in the eastern states continues to ignore the past, and do not talk with each other about his sexual preferences.
- Another couple has decided to stay together. He, gay, claimed to her that he was not sexually active, but confiding in me, privately, made it clear that he continued to find partners.
- A wife, now deceased, had a secret affair with a woman in Pittsburgh. Her friends who knew her were often angry that she had dumped her lover, and that she was not honest with her family.

In writing this letter, I am making no recommendations or offering no advice. I am not suggesting steps that you ought to take. Your story, Anne, simply caused me to do some reflecting and I thought I would share the thoughts with both of you. Perhaps I have made assumptions about your relationship. That is not what I intend. I wish the very best for each of you and the two of you, now and in the future.

Love,
Ralph

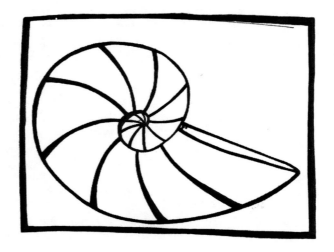

On Coming Out

A number of years ago I attended a lesbian and gay support conference in Breckenridge, Colorado. Two of the speakers shared the presentation and talked about three phases of coming out: personal, private and public. It was noted that the phases overlap each other and are interwoven with each other. It was also noted that one moves back and forth through the different arenas – sometimes focusing on one phase and sometimes focusing on another.

Their approach has been helpful to me for years – and I hope that this reflection may be helpful for others.

Personal

When I was a boy I started to become aware of my sexuality. I had an attraction for other boys. But I came to this awareness slowly. My early talking to myself was simply 'It's okay. It is only natural.' In other words, I defined it as a part of my normal growing up. In fact, my father had given me a small book entitled "Growing into Manhood." The content included non-judgmental paragraphs on sexual desire, masturbation, pubic hair, body image for the growing boy, and other thoughts that were important to me as a 13-year-old. I don't recall if there was anything on attraction to other boys or mutual masturbation. There might have been some expected opinions regarding sexual attraction to girls. I don't recall.

The struggle for any one of us seems to be, *how do I understand my own sexuality?*

For me the inner struggle has taken years. In my late teen years I read a few books, listened to the prejudiced faggot remarks of the boys in the halls

69

and in the shower room, focused on my fantasies, and generally felt very uncomfortable and unhappy with myself. And I felt lonely. Very lonely.

At times I still feel that in regard to myself – and as I consider other lgbt persons – I am homophobic. That is, I have biases about gays that I also put on myself. All of us - straights and gays - need self-awareness. My discomfort with myself comes up regularly.

What can be done to help me on this personal journey of self-understanding?

I must continue to recognize that it is personal. My searching and exploration into my own life and feelings are essential. And the internal probing is never done. The self-examination will be done when I am no longer conscious.

Others can help me understand my personal interior feelings, biases and self-blindness. Certainly as I write this and other articles, my own experiences and thoughts do, in some way, make the writing more subjective than objective. As my friends and family support and love me, they will, from time to time, help me explore the hidden agendas of my own reflections.

Private

When I was struggling with this personal journey I found that it was very helpful to share, on occasion, with family and friends. That, too, was a slow process. I recall that one day, in the early part of my journey, I talked with Chuck Boyer. He listened. And because he listened I grew stronger emotionally. I found that I loved and accepted myself just a little more because I was willing to share with him – and he listened.

Sharing with the family was not at all easy, but it was very important to do so, and it also strengthened my self-confidence. There were several family coming-out sessions. An early one was sitting by the Christmas tree with our children home from college, relating my story as best I knew it at the time.

The year following the Christmas tree story telling, our extended family had gathered for Thanksgiving. In the company of the adults I told them of my new understandings of myself as bisexual. They received my story openly. Again, it was a time of growth for me in self-understanding.

We McFadden brothers are a part of a cousin's chain letter. Though the cousins know that I have a partner I sometimes find it a struggle to bring them up-to-date on our home, our trips or our gardens. However, I have recently decided that even though some of the cousins are very religiously and politically conservative, I must, in order to honor myself and Keo, keep them updated on our activities. Now I send pictures, tell stories about our recent Laotian trips, and talk about our family activities. Frankly, I still get very little response – positive or negative.

Straight and gay – we find that we become more courageous when we share with family and friends our insights and thoughts. Sometimes – yes, even for straight folks – it is difficult, for instance, at a family gathering to let them know that you support gays or lesbians having a union service. Yes, I know, at family reunions we don't talk religion or politics. But think about it. Our families and friends can grow in wisdom and knowledge if they know what we are thinking and feeling.

While working as a chaplain with Hospice of Metro Denver, I had numerous conversations with parents struggling with the issue of how to tell their families that their son was gay and had AIDS. Perhaps it would not be accepted by their families, but they, as parents, grew in strength and insight when they found the courage to let others in the family know what was going on in their lives.

Public

This is the difficult one. When do I let the public know that I am gay? Even writing this book is yet another public coming out. I recently had a job with Hospice of Northeastern Illinois. I worked with a half dozen chaplains. There was an appropriate time when I came out to them. Was it difficult for me? A little. I wondered; would I lose my job or lose respect with the team of nurses, aids, social workers and office staff? Perhaps. But I have realized that a public coming out is becoming easier and easier. And each time I tell the truth publicly it is good not only for those who hear but also for me.

And how about you? I could give numerous accounts of gays and lesbians who have confided to me and to each other of how tired they are of straight people *privately* saying how much they support gays or lesbians, but are unwilling to be public about their support.

I would like to suggest that you consider, in a public forum, how you can be more supportive. At work, in a letter to the newspaper, at a rally or fundraiser for a gay organization – please consider being more public. You can come out as an ally and discover the courage, growth, and self-understanding lgbt persons have discovered by coming out.

It's so Simple, Isn't It?

A congregation, often called the Body of Christ, a community of believers, professing to be followers of Jesus, easily and frequently and simply says "All are welcome - to worship, to share in communion, to participate in outreach and service, to support and be supported." Yet that community may not quite know, because of fear, what the barriers are to opening their arms to a man who has, as partner and friend, another man.

I think, really, "It is so simple, isn't it?"

That man, with his partner, owns a home. He works at a job, has a salary, contributes to his college, and would contribute to the church if he could be received affectionately and openly. He is so 'common.' He doesn't like it when the winter adds additional cracks to the driveway. He wonders how long the American elm in the yard will survive. He is a careful driver who on occasion has a glass of wine but is never close to being tipsy. He is dangerously close to being 'normal.' Yet some of that Body of Believers have an inordinate fear of him. It makes no sense.

"Why?" I wonder. "It is so simple to be accepting ... isn't it?"

Most of the followers of Jesus are reminded that the greatest commandment is to love the Lord your God with heart, mind, soul, and strength and your neighbor as yourself. Yet some of these folks cannot condone or accept or love this man who is so like them. He can enjoy music they enjoy, cook brats on the grill, occasionally get excited by an NFL game, make a weekly trip to the library to check out another P.D. James mystery, but because his housemate is another male, the church members – like the culture around them – cannot commit themselves to being an open and receptive congregation.

Yet it is so simple to understand ... isn't it?

That mans works in a nationally known industry and he is promoted because he is loyal, has talent and experience, and that company, perhaps for financial or ethical or moral reasons, provides partner benefits for him and his companion. They, along with an increasing number of national companies, universities, and health care organizations, recognize and value the long-term commitment that some couples have. They know, just as clearly, that stable relationships add strength to their work. Strange then, isn't it that a "company of believers of Jesus Christ, who believe that they should do justice, love mercy and walking humbly with their God," remain exclusive?

I think that it is simple to understand and accept lgbt persons. It is simple ... isn't it?

Isn't it?

Being Dispirited

From time to time I recall a few lines from the chancel drama, "Christ in the Concrete City" by P.W. Turner. Jesus, with his disciples, has come to the garden to pray. He goes off a little ways, leaving them his instructions: "Wait here while I go and pray."

> A dialogue between the disciples arises:
> "Why does he tell us to wait? Is there nothing to do but
>   wait?"
> "Watch and pray that you do not enter into temptation."
> "Those were his instructions."
> "Watching is hard work when you do not know what you
>   are watching for."
> "Praying is hard work when you do not know what you
>   are praying for."
> "And cold work too, here in the darkness."
> "And in the loneliness."
> "How far away God seems when you are dispirited,
>   And tired,
>   And afraid."[6]

I wrote, one day, in my journal, "I am dispirited, and tired, and afraid."
   I am tired, tired sometimes of simply being.
      I want to be okay, without these feelings of despair.
         I have very little hope.
      I have very little energy for advocacy

---

6   P.W. Turner "Christ in the Concrete City," 1967, Radius

I say that my Source of energy and spirituality is the Inner Light, yet I have little awareness, really, of that Inner Light. There seems to be no place to find hope and security. For me, there is no source of life.

I want to escape from responsibility: to retire from advocacy, from being prophetic, and from taking on the really tough justice issues.

I am tired, dispirited, and afraid.

I want to escape. Escape from the church. I want the church to do something wrong so that I have a legitimate reason for leaving. I don't want to take the responsibility or decision on myself.

I want to leave. I am tired of this battle.

Part of the picture is that I am getting old and I don't care to do much of anything. I admit that I am not feeling 100% about myself. Too much homophobia by others and therefore, sometimes, about myself.

The continuous hate, fright, and fear projected by conservatives are almost overwhelming.

The way out is to leave the church or at least certainly try to forget about the denomination. The conservatives keep threatening to stop paying or to leave. Many of the progressives have stopped paying and have left.

What feeds my spirit?
Quietness.
Listening to my Soul, even as it says to me, fight and put up a struggle.
Determining that it is imperative that I tell the truth as I understand it.
Recognizing that I have a full life, and may have many years to live.
Even though I may wish to be in a cocoon, it is important that I believe in myself.
The love and caring of family and friends, many of whom are in the congregation.
Living with the interior faith and belief that
"There are many roads to go
And they go by many names.
They don't all go the same way
But they get there all the same."[7]
Some songs of David such as
"The Lord is my light and my salvation.
Whom then shall I fear? Of whom shall I be afraid?"
Psalm 27:1

---

7   Paul Colwell "Where the Roads Come Together," 1971, Up With People

Normalized or Demonized

I like mashed potatoes and gravy.

I don't like having more cracks in our concrete driveway.

I like the deep colors of our fall mums.

I prefer eggs over-easy.

I'm glad that I graduated from college.

Taking chaplain training in my late fifties was painful but fulfilling.

My high school years were sometimes lonely.

Our marriage was really very good.

I love golden Aspen leaves in October in Colorado.

Driving long distances with the CD playing is relaxing.

I take my turn cleaning the bathrooms.

I try to do my taxes honestly.

I am sort of computer literate.

I like my jeans when they are freshly laundered.

My handwriting is dreadful, especially compared to my father's artistic penmanship.

I sometimes eat too much of the wrong stuff.

I laugh at good comedians.

As I get older my singing voice wobbles more.

I really am tired of being in the hospital so often.

I'm pretty normal, right?

So why am I, because I am gay, identified as abnormal and sinful by some? Am I really that different? Who has the right to vilify? What are they afraid of?

There are times that I definitely want to be 'normal,' not outside the norm. I get tired of being considered 'odd' or 'queer' or 'strange' or 'weird' or 'abnormal.' I don't wish to be demonized by those who say that they love the sinner but not the sin. I don't care to be, as a civil and gracious and personable man, nonetheless, 'different.' And I sometimes feel like folks want me to be a "poster boy" of what a good gay man is really like.

On the other hand, I definitely want to be different and unusual and outside the norm when it comes to being an advocate for justice, peace, and compassion. I expect that a person who understands the life and ministry of Jesus is, compared to a lot of people, rather peculiar.

If normal in this culture is being nationalistic, materialistic, and self-absorbed, then I don't want to be normal. If normal is not recognizing or not doing anything about hunger or war or rotten politics or injustice to minorities, then I do not want to be normal.

So probably even as a gay man, I do not want to be normal.

Neither do I want to be demonized. But as a progressive disciple, I may be demonized by some. I will be demonized because I do not fit the norm.

On the other hand (is that the third hand?), there are, thankfully, those who are attempting to normalize (i.e. put into a somewhat acceptable common perspective) the daily lives of those who have been marginalized because they are lgbt folks.

American industry, universities, and health care organizations are increasingly including partner benefits within their hiring policies, carrying out in-house anti-discrimination education, and advertising products for the public that show inclusive relationships.

These groups, agencies, and companies are working to normalize the lives of lesbians, gays, bisexuals, and transgender persons. These groups, with significant self-study, debate, and open dialogue, are letting the lgbt folk know that they want sexual orientation issues to be non-issues.

Often the churches locally, regionally and nationally are lagging far behind those secular agencies.

Some churches and some denominations - evangelical, conservative and more progressive - are trying to keep the money coming in and their churches growing by playing to the prejudices of the public. Yes, they believe it is an issue of theology, but in my view they haven't tried very hard to gain a perspective that is more religious and less cultural.

Some pastors, church executives, and national staff, although they say that they support lgbt persons and issues, demonize and abuse by their silence those same persons. And the result of their silence is that they, unwittingly, stand with those who are openly, verbally abusing and demonizing lgbt persons.

I am thankful that over the years of being more and more open I have also thought of myself as an 'okay person.' I am, in terms of the over six and a half billion people in the world, pretty much normal. And yet I am also unique. I am thankful for the complexity and yet the simplicity of my life.

So I guess that makes me pretty normal . . . right?

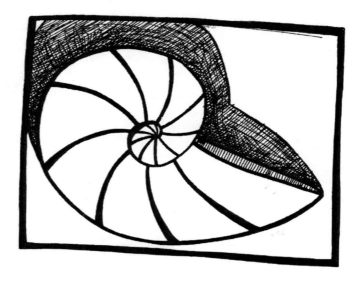

Gadfly

My father was courageous, wasn't he? After the Second World War he and my mother invited Japanese Americans into our home when it was definitely not acceptable. He invited a black family to be members of the Troy Church of the Brethren in the 1940's. He helped to open up equal housing in Elgin.

I am motivated, at times, to be an advocate. In the early 1990's I was hurt and angered as I spent time with young gay men with AIDS, who were trying to deal with parents unwilling to accept their son's sexual orientation or illness ... not telling relatives, not telling their church friends or business friends, afraid to touch their son as he lay dying, unwilling to learn about the disease, and sometimes speaking their certainty about sin and hell. One particularly difficult time for me was when a mother would not allow her son's long-time lover to attend the memorial service. He and his friends had their own service at another time. I was glad that they asked me to lead the service.

On the other hand, there were individual stories of courage and change that personally motivate me to be more courageous:

Parents who finally told their school teacher friends and church friends of their gay child.

Parents who embraced the partner of their dying son and tried to understand his hurt.

Parents who started teaching others.

Individuals who became active in AIDS and gay support groups.

I am motivated, I know, by the actions and thoughts of others. Writer Michael Robotham wrote in his book *Suspect*, "I was so worried about rocking the boat that I failed to spot the iceberg."

BMC Executive Carol Wise wrote to the participants on the Voices for an Open Spirit website, "With all due respect, I would, gently, suggest that an action step is frequently missing on the Voices for an Open Spirit* list. Although the call to patience and continued dialogue sounds like a great 'third way,' it ignores the very real situation of lgbt people, which is that they uniquely face ongoing and persistent discrimination while the 'dialogue' continues unabated. I am reminded of Martin Luther King Jr.'s comment directed at William Faulkner: 'It is hardly a noble act to encourage others patiently to accept injustice which he himself does not endure.' "

The fact is, I know on this cold January 27, 2009 day, that I am now very willing to write and be an advocate. Perhaps because the culture is changing so quickly it is too late to try to make a difference . . . yet there are hundreds of thousands who still are very unclear, very uneducated, and very prejudiced. Education is needed. Change is still very much needed.

Yes, it is okay to be a gadfly, an annoying person. I can do what it takes to make a difference. I am thankful that many who have gone before me were gadflies. They have made a difference in my life.

"We need, in every community, a group of angelic troublemakers." Bayard Rustin

* VOS - See Glossary

Control

Something was learned on our recent trip to Laos … something I should have realized a long time ago but possibly sidestepped on purpose. The following is a quote from my journal.

It is 2:30 Sunday afternoon, March 30, 2008. This evening we start our return trip to the United States. I realize that I can hardly wait. I am having a difficult time being patient. I am anxious. I am almost afraid. Yes, I guess I can say that I am afraid. What if the plane doesn't fly tonight? What if we are late getting into Bangkok and miss the Korean Air flight? I don't ordinarily become this anxious, but sometimes it does happen. (Like the time I blew up at the church board meeting. But that's another story… and yet it is also connected.)

We have been here in Laos for nearly four weeks.

I am constantly in the presence of persons who speak only Laotian. With Keo's help I can get an interpretation of what is going on, but I must always rely on his translation. Otherwise I can only guess at what is being said. The conversation, the laughter, the comments, and the decisions often go on without my understanding or participation.

I am in a land that I do not know. The weather is dry and hot, though sometimes humid. The air is hazy and often smoky. I wake in the morning to the unusual: under a mosquito net, hearing roosters crowing, and seeing the beginnings of the haze caused by countless coals being stirred into fires for the morning heating of coffee and cooking of breakfast.

While I am here I buy peanut butter, jelly, cheese slices, and soft white bread. I eat eggs in the morning, drink bottled water, and bathe by pouring cold water over my head. Throughout the visit, I am very careful about what I eat, because I may get sick with diarrhea.

I have a chronic platelet disease. It is currently inactive. Each morning I check my tongue and cheeks to see if there are any blood spots. I think carefully about what I will do if the ITP symptoms should come back again. I consider how we would get to Bangkok, get to the hospital, and take care of the luggage and changing tickets.

I have found myself counting the weeks and days. Often. How many days have we been here? How many days until we leave? I have kept track of the days in a notebook, carefully noting each passing day. Only 12 more days, 11 more days, or 10 more days. Halfway through. At times, the clock seems to quit moving.

And then, this morning, the last day and the last hours, it all seems to come to a head. I am anxious. I am almost distraught. I cannot relax. I remind myself to breath, but it doesn't seem to make a difference.

And then the insight. All of this time here I have had almost no control. I am asked, on occasion, what I want to eat. Or not eat. I am asked if I want to go along with the others to the market. I am asked what I want to do. But the decision is reached without much conversation on my part. It's not wrong, it's just that I sometimes have very little to do with it.

This morning, worried as I am about getting to the airport, I find out that we will go to the relative's home, and stay there until time to go to the airport. In the meantime, Keo's brother's family is still getting ready. It will probably work out okay. But at home in Elgin I decide when and how we would get to the airport. It's entirely up to me. I arrange the transportation. I buy the tickets. Keo decides what clothes and suitcases to take, but I make the major decisions along the way.

Here in Laos, I have been and I am frustrated. And anxious. And, yes, fearful.

March 30, 2008

It is three months later, and I am again wondering about control. On June 1, I was hospitalized with an infection. That day my gall bladder was removed. A couple of days later I returned home, a little sore, but okay. I was out of the hospital in time to get back to work facilitating interviews of the five candidates for an executive position. As of noon that Saturday my official job was done.

Two weeks passed without incident, but on the second Saturday following the gall bladder operation the infection returned and I had to return to the hospital. Days went by as the staff attempted to find out more about the infection. Blood draws, blood cultures, colonoscopy, echocardiogram, transesophageal echocardiogram, coronary CT angicardiogram, ultra sound on abdomen and on the throat, check ex-rays, an EKG, and finally, it seems, open heart surgery to replace an infected aorta valve.

All of this time, the doctors and nurses have tried to keep me up on the procedures, what will occur, when it will happen, how long it will take, and what the side-effects may be. At a certain time in the process it became clear that there would be the open heart surgery. It was delayed once for four days because of a weekend and because another procedure for someone else took precedence.

Looking over my daily life now – as I grow older, as I deal with a life-threatening disease, as my work roles are changing, as I realize that my life is moving along at an alarming rate, and as I realize that I will, in the next number of years, die. I know that at least one of the issues I am dealing with now is control.

I have little control over my aging. I can exercise, do fast walks, watch what I eat, and go to the doctor. But my body and mind are getting older. My skin sags. I seem to have a problem with short-term memory. On occasion I have a problem with balance.

I have little control over the ITP. I can be careful about what drugs I take. I can be aware of food intake and nutrition. However, the original source of the ITP and its occasional return are difficult to trace.

I have some control, but very little, in having fulfilling work. I am lucky, I think, to have had this short-term executive search job that started six months ago. I readily admit that it gives my life value. I need to look at that fact closely. After the search is over, then what? Will I look, as I have in the past, for another paying job?

I am being paid now for being a personal assistant, for custodial work, and for this executive search job. I say that I want to have the time to write. But I keep very busy doing something else.

I have control over my time, but I allow time to be taken from me. Church board work, mentoring, personal assistant, the search process, custodial work and interviews on mortality. . . life goes on.

I have learned during this long hospital stay to take the time ... to journal. To call family and friends. To receive family and friends in the hospital room. To read something new. To take notes on what was happening. To, as much as possible, declare some degree of independence. To walk in the halls often. To treat the staff kindly. To eat carefully. To drink plenty of water. To take the time to bathe, to brush my teeth. Instead of unquestioningly wearing the open back "everyone can see my rear" gown, to wear my soft leisure pants and a tee-shirt. In effect, to have as much control over my daily life as possible.

My own prayers and the prayers of others do have an effect on me. Hopefully, the prayers and the anointing service I have had will reduce my anxiety so that I am ready when one day this week the surgeon will cut open my chest in order to prolong my life.

June 30, 2008

Postscript

I have had, over the last two decades, increasing control over what to say and how to feel about my own sexual orientation. The church may wish to control my attitudes and activities by preaching, teaching, and innuendo. However, though I recognize that there is much that I do not have control of, I do have the willingness to be open about my sexual preference. Out of respect for myself and other lgbt Christians, I wish to be an advocate for truth, justice and equality. These are, I know, values I have learned as a follower of Jesus.

Remembering a Water Buffalo

I would like to introduce you to my partner, Kongkeo Xayavongvane.

Keo was raised in Selak, a small village just south of Savannakhet, one of the larger cities in Laos. During his childhood and into his teenage years, he was surrounded by a family of his father and mother, three brothers, and three sisters. Together they played with relatives and friends not only from their own village but also in near-by villages. And they worked, even as children, as soon as they were able, on the family farm – a property of rice paddies.

Recently, when Keo and I visited the village of his birth, he reminded me as we saw children playing on the dusty yard, that I could see him as a boy, for, he noted, in some ways very little had changed. The little girls helped to carry water on their shoulder yokes, helped to cook and keep the fires burning, and sometimes played with their toys. The little boys brought in firewood, dug for insects in the ground for dinner that evening, and moved the cows or water buffaloes to different places for grazing. They occasionally were allowed to go fishing. The children – boys and girls – walked on the dusty dry streets to school, and either came home for lunch or carried a woven basket with sticky rice and perhaps a couple of green vegetables. On those same streets they played games tossing their sandals toward a target circle, or playing a form of kick-ball. I could see Keo there 45 years ago ... dirty feet, dirty face, dirty shorts ... and, as Keo, said, contented. He knew no other life.

As a part of the farm, the family owned water buffaloes. Keo's job, often, was to lead the water buffalo as it pulled a plow or cultivator through the water and mud of the rice paddy. And sometimes it was possible, both for pleasure and for work, to ride on the back of the animal, clutching its massive back with his bare knees and hanging on to the strong broad neck. Because the water buffalo was slow, deliberate, and gentle, it was not dangerous. It was, in fact, pleasant and fun.

Now fast forward through the early years. Keo's mother died when he was only ten. He and his family took on even more responsibilities. And there was always school. In his early teens, Keo went into Savannakhet to live with his brother and attend the upper grades. He rode his bike to school. He had friends his own age and roamed over the growing city. For leisure and for a little spending money he, along with his friends, sold lottery tickets alongside the road. Once in awhile he and his family and friends would enjoy a festival for raising money for the monks of the local wat (temple).

And there were always the wars. Laos was often in conflict with its neighbors who wished to add Laotian territory to their own nation. Keo's misfortune was to be raised at a time when there were conflicts all over Indo-China in Viet Nam, Cambodia, and Laos. The communists of Viet Nam used the northeastern edge of Laos for the Ho Chi Min Trail. And when the United States left Southeast Asia, the government, the People's Republic of Laos, supported the invasion by Communists and encouraged Communism in the nation. Keo recalls being a young teen in Savannakhet, hearing and seeing the Communist helicopters and bomber planes take off from and land on an airfield.

In 1975 Keo and his younger brother, Ko, as anti-communists and, for the most part, unsuccessful guerillas, found it necessary to flee their home and country. Keo, during the rainy season and despite the flooded Mekong River, with the aid of a banana tree log, escaped from Laos by swimming across the Mekong River at night. He ended up for three years in a refugee camp in Thailand. He was then transferred to Houston, Texas, for placement. Because a friend had moved here and the YWCA was willing to sponsor him, Keo landed in Elgin, Illinois.

Fast forward again through almost twenty years: language classes, work in a factory and in hotel housekeeping and supervisory roles, and, then, illness. But despite the major shift from village to city, from playing children's games in the dust in the village to TV's, sports cars, and fast food, Keo adapted to this new culture, as did his brother and many Lao friends. Elgin and the United States became home for thousands of Laotians. Within the last few years, through classes, tests, interviews and patience, Keo became a citizen of the United States.

His life has included traveling to new states by car and by plane. He came to Colorado early in our relationship, and we visited Rocky

Mountain National Park, Yellowstone National Park, the Tetons, and the Grand Canyon.

A humorous story captures some of the contrasts of his life. Following one of those vacations, Keo returned home to Elgin from Denver, and was picked up at the airport by a friend. Getting home brought back the reality of day-by-day living. As he arrived back at his apartment parking lot, he checked on his car. Oh, no! A flat! What a welcome home!

Two days later, because of a change in signs at an intersection near his apartment, he made an illegal left turn. His reward was a $100 fine. That's two.

And again, two days after that, driving back from the grocery store, his car was hit – right rear – by a vehicle trying to 'hurry' an intersection. That's three.

That evening, unhappy and sad, he called me in Denver. He related the events of the week. He sighed. His frustration was evident. Perhaps with a longing for the simpler life and wondering how it was back home in Laos, he sighed deeply and reflected, "Sometimes I wish I was riding a water buffalo."

Keo and I have traveled to Laos four times in the last ten years, experiencing the extreme contrasts between the United States and Southeast Asia. And one of the most significant differences I have experienced is in the religious attitude of Christians and Buddhists. Keo is Buddhist, as are his family in the United States and Laos. Yet in Laos or with his Laotian Buddhist friends in the United States, I/we feel no threat, no judgment, and no rejection because of our relationship.

Keo is a remarkable person: sensitive, strong, clever, funny, and loving and he deserves no less than full acceptance. I am very proud and glad that he is a part of my life.

The Leaves are Falling – and *Monk*

Today Keo and I raked leaves. A lot of leaves. And this was the fourth time with another time or two to come. We have three giant oaks, a sugar maple, three varieties of crabapples and a weeping willow. The oaks have almost finished the cascade for this year. There are a few old dried-up leaves that are the die-hard types, hanging on until next year when the young come along and push the old off. (That metaphor is a bit unsettling for this aging man in his seventies.) The maple is sort of casting off the remnants whenever it feels like it, and the weeping willow simply can't get around to realizing that it is November.

As we raked I was reminded of several things. Have you watched the TV show *Monk*? Wonderful show! Monk is a self-employed detective with obsessive-compulsive disorder. A perfectionist in every detail. It is with his intelligence and intuition that he solves the unsolvable.

As we raked I shared with Keo my vision of what it might be like for Monk to rake leaves on a day like today. We laughed. Gloriously sunny and windy day with the leaves still peppering the ground. I could just see Monk putting all the leaves in a large paper lawn bag (that's the way we have to do it in our neighborhood), and then scurrying here and there, frustrated as he grabs one falling leaf at a time almost before it hits the ground.

At times my life is like the raker of this afternoon. I can rake and pull together the leaves and stuff them in the paper bag and (unlike Monk), if the wind blows a few around, or a tree keeps letting the golden yellow and dark and light brown bits float or blow to the ground, I don't mind. It's okay. There is always another day. I just go ahead and enjoy the warmth of the sun on my face. Besides, I know that I will win one day. Most of the leaves will be raked and bagged. It's okay.

That's how I feel sometimes about the endless political debates about who has the most experience, the wisest insights, the best idea of what "the people" really need, and who will best get us out of Iraq. Let the powerful discuss and argue their points. I conclude – it's okay! Let the seasons change. Let the old dry leaves succumb to the natural cycle of life and death. Let the fresh growth come. It's okay. I am content – for tomorrow is another day. As has been said, "This, too, will pass."

At other times, I confess, I am like Monk. By golly, I want the leaves all to be in one place and to stay in place. Once I have it all taken care of, then let it be. I know how I want my life to be. I know how life is. The endless 'dialogue' frustrates me. I want solid, fulfilling, developed, truthful, and concrete answers. I want the paper lawn bag filled and closed.

Moral of the story? I guess the fall will be. And the politicians and moral soothsayers will be. No easy answers. Always some loose leaves. And even those who say that they know the future.

Thankfully, I have learned that there is something beyond autumn. In the cycles of life and of politics, winter follows autumn, and then, God bless us, we will be refreshed with a brilliant new spring.

And just as I know that spring will come, so I have hope that our leaders, some already chosen and some yet to be elected, will bring, just as spring promises, new hope and new life. No easy answers, not all the leaves carefully placed in the bags. But, perhaps like Monk, an authentic solving of the unsolvable. And then, I know, fall and the scattered leaves will come again.

Mt. Evans at Timberline

Mt. Evans at timberline with the grand old crones and sages -
   survivors, gnarled, fire-scarred, bent with the shape of
   the centuries of age and wind, among boulders coated
   with grey and green lichen, and the tundra, quilted with
   golden, yellow, sky-blue, white, bronze, red, and violet -
   summer conquerors of a deadly winter,each one amazed
   at its own returning to the land of the living.

All - trees, stones, flowers, grasses - perched here within the endless ranges
of towering might and majesty -
      and with some of the granite giants still harboring
      inlets of August snow from last spring's heavy pack.
A mystical place!
      I've been here before. Often.
      To sit on grass or needles or rock.
      To know that here on these quiet secluded slopes lay the
         ashes
      of two men - one in his fifties and the other in his seventies.

Larry died early and his family scattered his ashes while the bagpipes -
   two hundred yards away, dirging an ancient plaintive
   mountain melody called us to consider our mortality.
And Harold - whose family lived in West Virginia - only asking that his
   wishes for his ashes to be scattered in the mountains be carried
   out, and I chose this sacred ground because I knew it.

The ground has received the ashes - and two winters have sucked them
  into the arid and shallow topsoil. Two men who lived with
  family and friends, who fashioned their lives around jobs,
  and sex, and wonderment about living.

Here I now sit on a hard unyielding boulder, its roughness imprinting
  my aging buttocks, aware but not able to comprehend, my
  own finitude, my miniscule being in a timeless infinite
  universe.

One day my ashes will join those scattered here on this ancient
  peninsula with weathered and whitened stones and pines.

One day - how soon? Will my death be simply another death and one
  day there being an energy of Soul - will my Light also
  be free of body — and, hopefully, free of this torment of
  uncertain being?

I can't comprehend it - soul without body - and what of mind —
  thinking - feeling?

I retreat to this haven - this place of the boundary of tree life at its last

I retreat - knowing that I am only a few seconds away from a road
  battered with tires and tourists and noises and yet -
  in the midst of this place - the only eternity I presently
  know.

An Ancient Survivor on Mount Evans
Photograph by Ralph McFadden

Beyond the Sunset

It's an open casket.
   Dorothy, peaceful and pain-free, silver gray hair,
   looking younger than her 89 years, dressed in a soft Wedgwood dress
   selected by her only son and his wife.
   When it's over the friends will say, "She looked lovely."

The service is over. As chaplain I sit in front, near the casket,
      facing the chapel pews, absorbed in the faces
      as the mortuary director encourages the friends
         about 40 of them – in their 70's and 80's –
      to pass by the casket, say last goodbyes to Dorothy
      and support the only son and his wife and their son
      with a tear, a handshake, a hug.

They come forward (last row always goes first) quietly -
      some frail, some slow, some with a cane, almost stoic,
      gazing on Dorothy's still and silent figure,
      recalling her lively sense of humor, and opinionated
      politics.

Missing her.

And consciously - or not - immersed in reflections on mortality and
      immortality.

   How long before I too may no longer be here?
   How will I look? And who will care?
      Will it hurt? What if there is too much pain?
      She looks so peaceful – thank God.

Will we have enough money for the funeral?
Even for the final days? Will it hurt?
This makes me so sad for her and for her family
. . . and for me.
Those are nice bouquets. Will there be many for me?
Oh, Lord, I miss Ben. Just two years ago.
It seems like yesterday. Will I see him soon?
Will I see him?
Am I ready to die? I don't like to think about it.
My, it feels warm in here. Will it hurt?
What do I say to her son? I haven't met him before.
Will my children really care? Really?
Why doesn't the line move? I want to get back to my room.
I must write to my daughter.
I wonder why I come to these funerals.
It seems like there have been so many recently.
So many gone.
Will it hurt?
I was glad for Dorothy. She was a good woman.
They said the right things.
I'll be okay when it's my time. It will be alright.
I think I'll have them sing "Beyond the Sunset."

Many Roads

Our father, W. Glenn McFadden was, in my estimate 'border line' - a borderline liberal. At times, some would shake their heads sadly and say, "Glenn had gone over the edge - he was addicted to liberalism."

That liberalism of my father may be in the family genes. In fact, my Mennonite mother was, in living out her faith, pretty liberal. We three sons of Glenn and Eva are all liberals and progressives to varying degrees. If you will excuse the term, I seem to be the most flaming of the three of us.

I have a recent illustration of that liberalism, defined by someone else.

In the May 2002 Church of the Brethren monthly periodical *Messenger*, there was an interview with the Paul Grout, the recently elected as the Moderator of the Church of the Brethren Annual Conference. If I read the interview of Moderator Paul Grout correctly, I may have to identify myself not as a liberal but as an ultra liberal. And it was a quote from Paul in his interview that set me on this reflection.

Paul said in the interview, "There is a liberal element in the church that really doesn't want Christianity. That thinks it doesn't make a difference whether it's Buddhism or Hinduism, and shouldn't make a difference because there really is no difference, because Christianity is seen as just one of many religions. That has done deep damage to the church. That is ultra-liberalism." Grout does go on to say "Ultra-conservatism has been just as damaging, perhaps more damaging to the church."

Paul Grout is saying that Christianity is the only way. The only truth. John – 14th chapter – seems to say the same thing. "I am the way, and the truth, and the life. No one comes to the Father except through me."

John was considered the most spiritual of the four gospel writers. He framed his theology strictly and narrowly. It might be also understood that such a fundamental approach was a needed source of strength for those who were persecuted in the early church, those he was writing for. Today, in an atmosphere of terrorism and suicide bombings, it is appealing to folks to believe that there is only one way – the way of the Christian. Or, depending on your upbringing, the way of the Muslim, or the way of the Jew.

A former denominational moderator of our denomination, Desmond Bittinger, gave a presentation in 1958 for the 250th anniversary celebration of the founding of the Church of the Brethren. It was entitled "And How Shall the Brethren Be Recognized?"

Bittinger wrote, in referring to a way to understand prayer, ". . . prayer no longer asks, 'Give me strength for my myself;' it does not even ask, 'Give me strength to do your will.' It humbly petitions, 'Give me an open mind to learn your will.'" Bittinger continues,

> This concept, it seems to me, is one of the major contributions of the Brethren to Christendom and to the world. This doctrine of the open mind and heart, I believe, lies at the very center of our faith. Our assurance is not that we know God's will; rather, it is that we are seekers after it, pursuers of it. We would not want to seem possessive at this point. Other Christians have held this point of view, also. But we as Brethren have made it central in our church. This is why we would never write a creed: We do not want to halt or slow down the quest for truth. (Founder) Alexander Mack wanted a major distinguishing mark of the Brethren to be an open, yearning mind, a mind forever searching for the will of Christ.

> This, then, is one of the marks by which the Brethren of the future shall be recognized: they shall be prayerfully searching for the truth, focusing upon the open Bible. I would not be true to my own mind, however, if I sought to confine the Brethren to the Bible only. God has ever been seeking to become manifest. God is left nowhere without a witness. The earnest, seeking Brethren or Christian of tomorrow will be able to discover the truth of God everywhere. It is

written in the stones, in the trees, in the minds and hearts of other people, in their unfolding lives and cultures.

I would even go further than this and say that some of God's truth is written in the holy scriptures of other religious groups. It is certainly found in the Hebrew scriptures of the Old Testament. It is also to be found in the Talmud, in the Koran, in the holy writings of every religion in the world.

Desmond Bittinger was suggesting a perspective that took adventure, courage, thoughtfulness, respect, insight, and wisdom.

I do not have to completely embrace what another believes. I do not have to become Hindu. I do not have to become Buddhist. But, it is my conviction, that as a Christian I do not have a corner on the truth. Christianity does not have all the truth. The Bible does not have all the truth.

For many Americans and Christians since the terrorist attack on the Twin Towers, there is a renewed effort to communicate and work with those of other faiths, especially Muslims. Why? What is being implied? Where are these dialogues taking us? I would hope that part of the involvement with other faiths is to discover truth, and not simply to be in conversation to defend our own perspective.

The fundamentalists of most faiths are angry with those of their own faith who will not claim, along with them, that their point of view is the only view worth having. To the fundamentalist, dialogue is a heresy. It is possible to talk with persons of other faiths, but only to persuade them that they are wrong.

Does inclusiveness and respect and love for diversity damage or free the church? For me, faith involves and includes inclusiveness, richness, completeness, flavor, extensiveness, comprehensiveness, breadth, and abundance. Faith is not a matter of building a wall to exclude those who worship Allah, or Yahweh, or the Great Spirit.

Are we so arrogant that we, with all of our weaknesses and uncertainties, can really believe that others, now and through the centuries and throughout the world, have no understanding of spirit, truth, human values, and creation?

Keo, my partner, is Buddhist. His English language skills are good, but not terrific. But while he may not be able to express his thoughts in perfect English, when understood he is very clear with his perspective and sometimes humorous. Recently we were talking about the rather large Lao community in and around Elgin. I mentioned the fact that there are several small Lao Christian churches. I asked if any of those Christians also, on occasion, attend the Buddhist festivals. The festivals draw hundreds of folks from a large region. He and his friends smile about some of the Lao Christians who have, cautiously, come to the festivals. At one festival a Lao Christian was heard to say that she was fearful about being at the festival because one time, when watching the festival parade, she was splashed with some of the monk's holy water . . . and she immediately got a headache. She exclaimed that as a Christian she was being punished for being present at a Buddhist ceremony. And then Keo added, "A Buddhist would never feel the same way about attending a Christian ceremony."

One Saturday in 2006 I conducted a memorial service for a Vietnamese woman. She was Christian and her family, for the most part, was Buddhist. The memorial included a Buddhist prayer service at 9:30 for the family and at 11:30 a Protestant chaplain's memorial service. Of interest to me was that the monks for the Buddhist ceremony were Lao, from an Elgin Lao temple. Again, the family was Vietnamese. They did not, for the most part, understand the chanted words of the Lao monks. But one of the Lao monks that I knew said to me following the ceremony, "It doesn't matter. It is the same Buddha."

How often I have heard those words from patients in hospice. When it comes down to the wire, the patient or family, being Catholic, or Methodist, or Baptist, or not currently participating in a church, will very often say, when asked about a prayer or a memorial service, "It doesn't matter. It is the same God."

A number of years ago, a choral group "Up With People" had as one of its focus pieces "Where the Roads Come Together" by Paul Colwell. It has lyrics that some may say are naïve. I like the lyrics. They speak volumes for an inclusive understanding of our humanity. Here are two verses.

None of us is born the same.
We don't know why, it's the way we came.
Every heart beats a little differently,
Each soul is free to find its way
Like a river that winds its way to the sea.

There are many roads to go
And they go by many names.
They don't all go the same way
But they get there all the same.
And I have a feeling
That we'll meet some day
Where the roads come together
Up the way.[8]

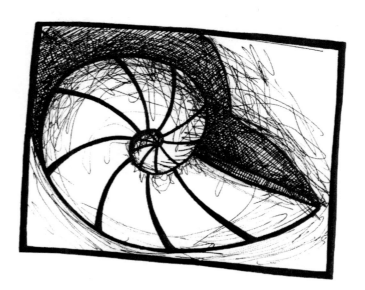

---

8   Paul Colwell, "Where the Roads Come Together" 1971, Up With People.

Faith is a Journey

Though I do not remember the year I do recall the feelings I had that day as I stood on the 10th floor balcony of a condo in Denver, Colorado. Two friends who had been leaders at the Church of the Brethren National Youth Conference in Ft. Collins had stopped by after the conference to visit and to deepen our friendship. Over the years I had learned to know them better and also knew that I could count on them for support. They were husband and wife. I had been one of the ministers at their wedding. In fact, the husband was one of the first persons that I had come out to many years ago.

Now I had a different confession in mind. I was going to 'come out' again, but on a different subject. And, in some ways, this confessional coming out seemed more difficult than the coming out as a gay man. For I was about to make a faith statement… or perhaps, it was a 'lack of faith' statement. I had and have serious questions about the reality of God's existence. And if there is doubt about God's existence, then that calls into question all manner of religious activity: prayer, worship, church attendance, religious education, quests for spirituality, endless writers and writings, the purpose of denominations, a history of personal family and church involvements, the meaning of seminary training, and so forth. My whole life has been built around the church. To consider this sea change is to consider a new type of isolation and aloneness.

As I type these words many years later I still feel the same cautiousness. I wonder who will eventually be reading these words. What will they think? And will they, my family and friends, put me on the fringe of their relationship because they cannot understand how I could have been a pastor, church professional and hospice chaplain, and still have had doubts about God's existence?

I have often reflected on my own faith experience on this life journey. When I was a judicatory church executive in the late 60's, at least one of my reasons for resigning from that position was not a mid-life crisis but a "faith crisis." Ten months later I resolved enough through self-examination that I returned to a professional church position.

When I was on the national staff of the Church of the Brethren, one of my faith explorations took me closer to the charismatic movement. I had a good friend in leadership of a charismatic fellowship group. I trusted him and cared for him. I was still married, but I trusted him enough to tell him that I was bisexual or gay. He listened, and while not twisting my arm, did encourage me to give myself in prayer to the Spirit. He did not say in that encouragement that he expected that I would give up my desires. I joked to myself –for I was an executive in the denomination – that it would be quite an announcement at our denomination's annual conference to come out publicly as gay . . . and charismatic. That did not, of course, ever happen.

This is all leading somewhere. In the early 90's when I was on the board of the Brethren Mennonite Council for Lesbian, Gay, Bisexual and Transgender Interests, one of the recurring agenda items was formal and informal goal setting as we defined our mission and our objectives. It became apparent over the months that our board members brought many differing ideas of what it was to be a part of the church. Of course, many of us were hurt, stung, and wounded, and our good intentions to be part of a congregation had been killed off by the very church to which we had given loyalty. That experience of the church was often reflected, personally, in our beliefs.

We found it difficult to be honest with each other. It was not about how we felt about the church or how it had impacted our participation in the church. We talked, with zeal, about the horrendous and cruel behavior of the church. But we realized that we could not come to any common agreement – even to disagree – about what we believed. Some were still attending a church. Some had long since separated themselves from the church and from a belief in God. Some still valued a church relationship and were persons who believed in prayer. Others had not only stopped going to church, but had also moved more toward being agnostic, and were a whole lot less prayerful.

We talked with each other about this phenomenon. We might confide individually but it was difficult to even suggest a theological discussion in which the board could take part. It was simply too sensitive a subject for some of us.

And now?

I don't know where most lesbian, gay, bisexual and transgender persons are.

On the part of some there seems to be a necessity to prove to the straight world that persons can be queer and Christian. 'The proof that I am an okay person, a whole person, is that even though I am gay, I am a person of faith. See my halo!'

At the other end of the continuum some will no longer spend time considering their spiritual lives. 'The church is a failure. I was left high and dry. I see no reward or helpful end-result by even thinking about my spirituality.'

For me it is different than that. I am a mature person (in this case mature means older) who has searched and continues to search the landscape of faith. And I have reached some conclusions, at least for the present. "For the present" implies that there is always the possibility of change. I like what Thich Nhat Hanh said: that when we were fifteen, we had a concept about the Buddha. Now we are older and we have a different perspective. And when we are yet again older, we will have yet another deeper point of view.

In thinking about and reflecting on my spiritual path and beliefs I find it helpful, primarily for myself, to note that I do have core values and beliefs.

I believe:

That most humans have a basic goodness.

That all humans have a shadow side.

That our "basic goodness" keeps our society from total destruction.

That most religions understand basic goodness – at least the founders did.

That, even so, much of follow-up religious teaching of the followers is destructive.

That when the shadow side shows itself, people hurt themselves and others.

That I cannot prove there is a god, and I do not wish to prove there is not a god.

That there is some truth in the Quaker 'inner light' within us.

That prayer may be effective, but it is because it works on
the inner self - The Soul.

That prayer can be destructive when it nourishes false
expectations.

That struggle is a good thing, at least for most folks.
(Sometimes struggle is so difficult that one ends one's
own life rather than going on and on with it.)

That it is important to live this life to the fullest. I wish
to live with respect for others and I do not consider it a
factor in my living whether I will or will not have an
after life.

Implications of what I believe:

That I have to check out my behavior regularly.

That I will respect my beliefs and myself.

That I will endeavor to respect the beliefs of others.

That I will live wisely.

That I will love wisely.

That I will try to live authentically.

That I will try to live each day with integrity.

That I will forgive myself for living inadequately and
incompletely.

That I will forgive others for living inadequately and
incompletely.

That I will think and live non-judgmentally.

That I will, however, speak openly of concerns of justice
for all persons.

That I will live joyfully and fully as long as I can.

That I will not extend my life when it is clear that my
health – emotional, physical, mental, and spiritual
– is not going to be with me much longer. In other
words, I have made end-of-life decisions and I will
expect my partner and my children to honor those
decisions.

At times, I am still on that 10th floor condo balcony. My coming out about faith is still confessional. And sometimes it is apologetic. Yet, I am in a much different place than I was fifteen years ago when I shared with my friends. I do not quake at revealing what I believe. In fact, I have discovered that when I have shared with others my pilgrim path they have, in turn, often expressed similar doubts . . . and the daily expressions of their finite faith. I am blessed when others share with me, and sometimes they seemed relieved that they are not alone in their faith journey.

Thankful for an Open, Affirming Congregation

In the fall of 2007, while chairing a church board meeting, I slammed my fist on the table and, in tears, shouted my anger and disgust. Then I stumbled and stormed out of the room and found the front door of the church. Wondering what had happened to my 'normal' careful and quiet disposition, I circled the church in a mood of frustration and disbelief. Within a few minutes, Cheryl, the vice-chair, was walking beside me and, saying nothing, assured me of her presence and support.

What had happened? In a business meeting in May 2007, after what seemed to me like an endless discernment and discussion process, the congregation supported by an 80 percent vote a resolution to welcome and include gays and lesbians. Now, in this board meeting a few months later, I felt that there were still those who wanted to skirt the issue by entering into yet more processes and more 'discernment' before we could really confirm our congregational action. I had waited, not very patiently, long enough, and when more questions of process came up, I blew up.

Now, about a year and a half later, to my pleasant surprise, I have sensed in myself a remarkable change. There is a certain stillness of spirit, a lessening of that internal anger that has been around for so many years. I find it difficult to name, but now I feel, to a much larger degree, that I belong in this congregation.

Part of the reason for the change in my spirit comes from the fact that recently the congregation agreed to become public with their resolution to be inclusive. This public openness would be with the district, the denomination, and the community. These past months I could see it coming and my spirit has been lifting. I feel that there is acceptance, understanding, and, for the most part, non-judging and unequivocal love. Many members, though not all, have come to share, as much as they can, the recognition that distancing and disenfranchisement is painful, hurtful, and wrong. They have decided that silence about who is included at the table is not acceptable.

Perhaps my feelings of peace also come from the fact that the congregation, despite the chaos of the culture, has, by its willingness to define justice for lgbt persons, confirmed my sense or desire that we are 'getting there' ...'there' being a growing awakening of equality and inclusiveness in the culture and in the broader church.

Why do I write this at this time? I am thankful. Yes, it is because the congregation has come to the place where it can willingly state its openness. But, in addition, this congregation is now a safe place for me and for other gays and lesbians.

Another important step came in May 2009 when the congregation voted to became a member of an international network of Church of the Brethren and Mennonite open and affirming congregations: the Supportive Communities Network, an ally of the Brethren Mennonite Council for LGBT Interests.

From my own experience and that of many others, it is a God-send to be a part of a congregation that is willing to not only accept lesbian, gay, bisexual, and transgender persons, but also has equipped itself to let the church and community know.

As I review the on-going life of this congregation, I realize that though the move to become a community that welcomes lgbt persons was difficult and strained at times, that movement was part and parcel of who we are.

For instance, in recent years there have been three lives, deaths, and memorial services that have had profound effects on my life and thinking and that of the congregation.

Each of these three women was beloved by family, friends, and the congregation. And at the time of the accidental death of one and the terminal illnesses and deaths of the other two, the family and close friends were deeply loved, embraced, cared for, and nourished by the congregation.

The spouses often remarked how they were almost overwhelmed by the compassion of the members and friends of the congregation. Of course, they also experienced the love of family and other friends. But the emphasis of this note is on the care of the congregation as a supportive, caring, and deeply involved community. This congregation has shown, over the years, an extraordinary compassion to care for loved ones at the time of death.

This past spring, summer and fall, the supportive care of the congregation was emphasized in another way - the dedication of four babies. The emphasis of the service was three-fold: to give a blessing for the child, to challenge the parents to provide support, nurture, and Christian upbringing, and to ask the congregation to affirm that they would stand by the parents, provide Christian education for the child, and be supportive as a community.

It is abundantly clear that each person and family in this congregation wishes to not only be a part of a community that gives, but also, when needed, wishes to be on the receiving end of that extraordinary support.

I think that our congregation is outstanding in providing support to those who experience crisis:

A death of a family member;

A teenager in trouble;

An older adult experiencing dementia;

A family member with a mental health concern;

A homeless person who comes to Soup Kettle (a Saturday night meal for those who hunger);

A stranger who is provided hospitality and support through the Narcotics Anonymous group that meets twice weekly in our facility;

A newcomer who is welcomed as he attends our worship service;

A widowed person who must make difficult decisions as she now lives alone in an empty house;

A recently separated or divorced person trying to reinvent his life;

A woman unemployed for the first time in her life;

A person hospitalized - either for normal health care, or for more serious life-threatening illness;

And it is also true that this congregation gives praise, thanks, and appreciation for:

A young person who reads scripture or plays an instrument for the prelude and offertory;

The folks providing coffee for the fellowship hour;

The members of choral groups and the pianists for services;

> An opportunity every Sunday in worship to name aloud ourselves, or those family members or friends who need our prayers;
> The teachers of children and adults;
> The volunteers for the Soup Kettle;
> The person leading worship; and
> The pastors who are visible in worship, teaching, and counseling.

Actually, the list of supportive and inclusive ministries is almost staggering. This congregation could take the very difficult and courageous step of becoming open and affirming of lgbt persons because it has had a history of reaching out, teaching, and acting justly toward all people, and living out the New Testament understanding of the life and ministry of Jesus. The mission statement of the congregation exclaims, "The Highland Avenue Church of the Brethren: a place to deepen faith, proclaim peace, embrace community, welcome others, and serve our neighbor in the compassionate spirit of Jesus!"

I have a deep commitment to this congregation – and I am thankful daily that this community is an open and affirming congregation in its many ministries. I recall that board meeting in the fall of 2007. I know that we and I have come a long way. I know that many congregations in our denomination have not come along this road, nor will they. But I and others can see a strong movement in the denomination and in other denominations toward a more inclusive and just agenda for all people.

My Prayer: To be Alive
as Long as I Live

I have always answered the doctor's office survey on "How is your health?" with a "5" or "Excellent." My family medical history is a bit more varied: my Dad died when he was 59 with a non-inherited multiple myeloma, which in English means a cancer that arises from a proliferation of a particular type of white blood cells, namely, the plasma cell. On the other end of the scale, Mom lived into her 90s. With Mom's good health and the fact that Dad's cancer was not inherited, I allowed myself the luxury of assuming, without really giving it much thought, that my health would always be good.

My son encouraged me to start running when I was in my early fifties. I eventually entered 5K and 10K runs. I recall being truly elated when, on a winter retreat, I ran on a golf course in sub-zero temperatures. As I reached my sixties and early seventies, it was hard not to be proud when people would say, "You don't look that old!"

The first challenge to my healthy self-image came in April of 2002. And it was a serious challenge – my first episode of immune thrombocytopenic purpura. ITP is a bleeding disorder in which blood has difficulty clotting due to an unusually low number of platelets. During that hospitalization I had a splenectomy. Apart from recovering from the surgery I did not, for the most part, feel sick. Then there was another ITP episode in 2005 and two more in 2007.

The reality for me, as I recall those many visits to the hospital, was that for the most part, I felt okay. Yes, I had a lot of IVs, pills, blood and platelet infusions, but as long as I was willing to walk with my tripod, I could go up and down the halls; I could use my borrowed laptop, and welcome visitors. How could I be as sick as I was being told I was?

Then, in the summer of 2008, my world was shaken when, due to an infection, I endured no fewer than four surgeries, including an ugly, bothersome and smelly colostomy. I felt that I had finally recovered from this when another round of ITP reared its head in April of 2009. This time I was warned that I could have a spontaneous brain hemorrhage. I try to keep a willing spirit.

Throughout these times there were several serious transitional issues.

When would I get through this ITP stuff, if ever?

Would that very serious infection attack again? When?

Was my will in order?

Was I prepared to die?

Did I have some thoughts about a memorial service
that I wanted my pastor and family to know
about?

During the last hospital stays and in the weeks that followed I lost volumes of muscle tone. My mid-section had become a patchwork of very poor quilting. My skin hung on protruding bones. I had literally become a belt-and-suspenders man, not by choice. By the time I got through 40 days in the hospital I had gone from 172 pounds to 135 pounds – leaving my 6 foot frame more than a bit skeletal. My self-image as a healthy man was seriously jeopardized.

I definitely was in transition. I was facing physical and emotional changes that I had not expected and was not prepared for. I was undoubtedly depressed at times. I found myself not wanting to see or talk with anyone, except a few family members and friends.

Early in 2008, before these surgeries, I had been working on a writing project related to my own thoughts and my 11-year hospice chaplaincy experience. That project included interviewing persons about their beliefs and attitudes about death and mortality. For a time I laid that project aside. I stopped looking at the obituaries; they made me uneasy – reading about persons in their seventies and eighties who had died. I must confess that I struggled with how much I wanted to live if it meant going through more surgeries.

Where am I now *in this journey?* There are several learnings, and I know there will be more:

+ Despite an underlying fear of a terminal illness
returning, I am determined to be alive as long as I

live. I walk daily, continuing to rebuild the depleted muscles and keeping my heart in tune. I see my doctors regularly to monitor my overall physical well-being and blood counts.

+ I am intentionally deepening relationships. Many of my family and friends and my congregation took extraordinary care to be in touch and to give me care. As a caregiver I was used to others being dependent on me; I didn't know how to be dependent on others. And, in spite of the gratitude I felt and still feel for the love and support I received, being on the receiving end of caregiving was not a comfortable place to be.

+ I must say that I have probably taken on a few new activities to which I should have said "no." This is something that I must deal with, fully acknowledging that it has much to do with feeling alive and of worth because I am doing something. Regardless, I will remain active. I am again working on writing projects, more determined to finish some of those tasks while I am able. However, my worth as a person is not simply in being more active. "Hyperactivity" is not the only way of assessing my life in the eyes of God or of friends!

+ I am thankful. I realize that I can be painfully sick, even without much physical pain. And I have a much deeper awareness of others who are in the midst of illness. Now more than ever I want to be sure that persons know that I care.

+ I am re-exploring the inner life. There is renewed spiritual awareness. One of the toughest issues for me is control: I wish to control my destiny, how I shall die and when. An artist friend helped me to recognize that I have no control. I can choose to be open to the flow of life. My life is in God's hands.

+ An important reminder of being open to the "flow" of life and of the Spirit happened three times during the course of my hospitalizations. My pastor and a few friends and family members came to my bedside for a service of anointing. I was awakened, through the anointing, to the simplicity of allowing the future to be what it will be - under the umbrella of the compassion of God's love, and the support and caring of the Community.

+ I do not wish to shy away from my aging, my life-threatening disease and my mortality. I have a friend who is a jazz guitarist to whom I said, one recent Sunday, that I wanted him to play for my memorial service. His response was, "Don't say that," and I realize that in my effort to be truthful with myself, I do not need to inflict that need on others. Part of a healthy response, for me, is putting in writing music, readings, and scriptures that I suggest be a part of my memorial service. My pastor now has access to a copy of my thoughts.

+ I realize, because I am uneasy about the subject matter, that I must find time to think mortality through for myself. I have not, in spite of these recent life-threatening events, been given a prognosis of imminent death. I do not know how I will react when that time comes. But because of the illnesses, I have been blessed with the time to reconsider my life journey. I am thankful for the remaining time in my life.

Psalm 139, a Psalm of David, is a favorite. The following are just a few of the verses from "The Message" translation.

GOD, *investigate my life; get all the facts firsthand.*
I'm an open book to you;
even from a distance, you know what I'm thinking.
You know when I leave and when I get back;
I'm never out of your sight.

Is there anyplace I can go to avoid your Spirit?
to be out of your sight?

Oh yes, you shaped me first inside, then out;
you formed me in my mother's womb.
I thank you, High God—you're breathtaking!
Body and soul, I am marvelously made!
I worship in adoration—what a creation!

The days of my life were all prepared
before I'd even lived one day.
Oh, let me rise in the morning and live always with you!

Investigate my life, O God,
find out everything about me;
Cross-examine and test me,
get a clear picture of what I'm about;
See for yourself whether I've done anything wrong—
then guide me on the road to eternal life.

Article from *Caregiving,* Caregiving Ministries Church of the Brethren
Edited copy, Volume 2, 2009

Glossary

BMC – Brethren Mennonite Council for Lesbian, Gay, Bisexual, Transgender Interests. Website: www.bmclgbt.org Carol Wise, who wrote the Foreword, is BMC Executive.

Church of the Brethren, National denomination. For information check their website: www.brethren.org.

CPE - Clinical Pastoral Education is an intensive training program in hospital and hospice settings, often in conjunction with seminary education. The author took his yearlong residency when he was fifty-five years old, many years after seminary.

Highland Avenue Church of the Brethren is the author's home church. Website: www.hacob.org

ITP - Immuno thrombocytopenic purpura is a bleeding disorder in which the blood has difficulty clotting due to an unusually low of number of platelets. Platelets (thrombocytes) are colorless blood cells that stop blood loss by clumping together at the site of a blood vessel injury and forming plugs in vessel holes.

LGBT is the contemporary alphabet soup for lesbian, gay, bisexual and transgender. More recently some have added Q . . . for queer. Queer is no longer demeaning but an acceptable term when used by the lgbt community. For the most part, lgbt when used in narrative is not in caps.

Messenger, Church of the Brethren national monthly magazine. For information their website is www.brethren.org.

Stonewall - During the last weekend of June of 1969, police and Alcoholic Beverage Control Board agents entered a gay bar--The Stonewall Inn, on Christopher Street, in New York City. Allegedly there to look for violations of the alcohol control laws, they made the usual homophobic comments and then, after checking identification, threw the patrons out of the bar, one by one. Instead of quietly slipping away into the night, as had been done for years, hustlers, drag queens, students and other patrons held their ground and fought back. Someone uprooted a parking meter and used it to barricade the door. The agents and police were trapped inside. They wrecked the place and called in reinforcements. Their vehicles raced to the scene with lights glaring and sirens blaring. The crowd grew. Someone set a fire. More people came. For three days, people protested. And for the first time, after innumerable years of oppression, the chant, Gay Power, rang out.

VOS – Voices For an Open Spirit, a Church of the Brethren informal group working for inclusiveness of all persons regardless of their theological point of view. With face-to-face dialogue it is possible for members of the church to find agreement to work together for the strengthening of the church.

Bibliography

Following is a list of resources that you may find of interest. *For Life is a Journey* only scratches the surface. If you would like to broaden your perspective and continue to build and move into a new nautilus chamber, take the time that is needed. Read one or more of the books listed. Check out the websites. Rent the 90 minute video *For the Bible Tells Me So* from your local library.

Books

Ellison, Marvin M. and Sylvia Thorson-Smith, Editors. *Body and Soul: Rethinking Sexuality as Justice-Love* [Cleveland: Pilgrim Press, 2003] Ellison and Thorson-Smith offer a broad and fascinating collection of essays from prominent theologians who are committed to an ethic that is inclusive of sexual justice.

Kreider, Roberta Showalter, Editor. *The Cost of Truth: Faith Stories of Mennonite and Brethren Leaders and Those Who Might Have Been* [Kulpsville, PA: Strategic Press, 2004] This powerful collection of personal stories from lgbt Mennonites and Brethren offers insights, understandings, and a powerful critique that the current "dialogue" about lgbt people often misses.

LifeQuest. *Taking a New Look: Why Congregations Need LGBT Members* [Fort Wayne, IN: LifeQuest Publications, 2008] Christian Community, a nonprofit research and resource development organization whose mission is improving the health of congregations and their communities, offers this booklet to initiate a conversation about the costs congregations and denominations face by not being welcoming and affirming of lgbt members. This resource may be downloaded at: www.churchstuff.com.

Lowe, Bruce W. *A Letter to Louise:* a 42 page free on-line treatise on Christianity and homosexuality. Can be downloaded at www. godmademegay.com.

Muller, Wayne. How, Then, Shall we Live? NY, NY. Bantam Books. 1996. One of my favorite books. Not lgbt focused. It raises the issue of how to live, knowing that one day we shall die.

Robinson, Gene. In the Eye of the Storm: Swept to the Center by God. NY, NY. Seabury Books. 2008. Robinson, as a gay man with a partner, was elected as Bishop of New Hampshire in 2003. Robinson and his parents are interviewed in the video, *For the Bible Tells Me So.*

Wallner, Mary Lou. The Slow Miracle of Transformation. Mary Lou travels over the United States, speaking out of the experience of the tragic death of her lesbian daughter, Anne. To purchase go to www.teach-ministries.org. Mary Lou is one of the interviewees in the video *For the Bible Tells Me So.*

Weiss, David. *To the Tune of a Welcoming God: Lyrical Reflections on Sexuality, Spirituality and the Wideness of God's Welcome* [Minneapolis: Mill City Publishing, 2008] David Weiss brings his theological training, poetic insight and activist passion to this collection of hymns, poems and essays that call the church to a full welcome of lgbt people

White, Mel. Religion Gone Bad, the Hidden Dangers of the Christian Right. Tarcher, 2006. Many of you know Mel White, author of Stranger at the Gate. Excellent and scary look at fundamentalism.

Websites

Human Rights Campaign. www.hrc.org. An excellent secular resource that includes updated information about religious agencies, industries, health care and higher education organizations.

National Gay and Lesbian Task Force. www.thetaskforce.org. Works to create a nation that respects the diversity of human expression and identity and creates opportunity for all.

Institute of Welcoming Resources, www.welcomingresources.org

Religious Institute on Sexual Morality, Justice and Healing, www. religiousinstitute.org.

Brethren Mennonite Council for LGBT Interests, www.bmclgbt.org.

Video

For the Bible Tells Me So: a powerful 90 minute video. A number of families and their lgbt children are interviewed. In-depth attention is given to understanding the authority of the Bible and homosexuality.